Destination
Tales from The Forbid

Destination Rum

Tales from The Forbidden Island

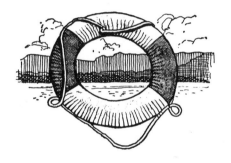

W R Mitchell

CASTLEBERG
2003

For
GEORGE LOGAN
who organised my first visit to Rum

A **Castleberg** Book.
First published in the United Kingdom in 2003.
Text, © W R Mitchell 2003.
The moral right of the author has been asserted.
ISBN 1 871064 23 6
Typeset in Garamond, printed and bound in the United Kingdom by Lamberts Print & Design, Station Road, Settle, North Yorkshire, BD24 9AA.
Published by Castleberg, 18 Yealand Avenue, Giggleswick, Settle, North Yorkshire, BD24 0AY.

Contents

In the Beginning 7

Road to the Isles 10

Brucie's Boat 16

The Bullough Connection 21

A Limping Pilgrim 26

First Impressions 30

Sir George's Dream House 35

Murderous Hordes 49

On the Tops 51

A Song of Rum 59

Kilmory Glen 61

Last Rites at Harris 63

Sea Eagles 67

Ashore on Eigg 70

Mission to Muck 77

Craking on Canna 80

Homeword Bound 86

Cover painting by David Hoyle.
Photographs by the author.
Drawings by Edward Jeffrey.

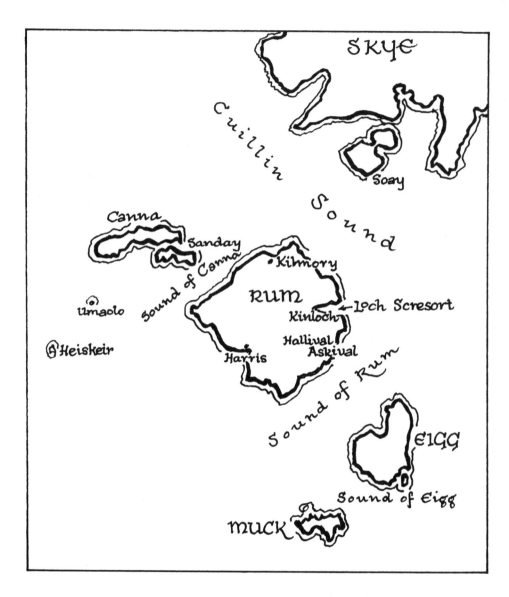

THE SMALL ISLES – drawn by Christine Denmead

In The Beginning

An untitled tape-recording that had lain in a bottom drawer for almost forty years began with a succession of clattering, wheezing, whirring sounds, followed by a fitful rendering of the march of the *Meistersingers*. Suddenly, remembering the circumstances behind the recording, I was transported to the island of Rum, and more precisely to the great hall of Kinloch Castle as it was late one night some thirty years before.

My friend George Logan – unmindful that most of our party of visiting deer-watchers were abed – was demonstrating the workings of a Orchestrion which, brass-piped and percussion-backed, reposed under the grand staircase. George slipped one of the perforated rolls into place, remarking: "Och – let's have Wagner." The Orchestrion, an Edwardian juke-box, was clearly in need of an overhaul. Wagner must have spun in his grave. When the Meistersingers had stopped marching, and I had switched off the recording, I half-closed my eyes and summoned memories of life on the Small Isles, in the Inner Hebrides, just south of Skye.

I saw Mallaig harbour, a mosaic of boats, with a torrent of silver herring cascading from a trawler under a gull-busy sky. The picture changed to one of the Sound of Sleet, flecked by silver light. Parties of shearwaters, oceanic birds newly returned from their wintering grounds off South America, skimmed the waves, waiting until dark before visiting their nesting burrows at the mountaintops of Rum. On the island, drake eiders bobbed on the flow-tide like two-tone buoys and crooned, *oo-ah*, a sound that Fred Smart, another of our islandgoers, likened to the sound of a duchess who had just had her bottom pinched. Oystercatchers, the pied pipers of a rocky, weed-draped shore, probed for food with beaks that were long and red, like sticks of sealing wax. Hooded crows, black and smoky-grey, picked up shellfish, rose into the air and dropped them on rocks to break the shells.

I brought to mind the great hall of Kinloch Castle, with its electrified organ and wooden balcony lined with the heads of what had been lordly red stags. Now bleached and glassy-eyed, they passed the long days gathering dust. I saw romantic paintings of Sir George and Lady Bullough as they were in their Edwardian prime. The skins of tropical animals and curios from the East testified to the Bulloughs' wanderlust and the fortune that had made it possible. In my own time, islanders who became friends included George MacNaughton, who ran the estate, and Ian Simpson, the ferryman, who could turn his hand to any sort of job.

Staying with Ian and his family at a house overlooking Loch Scresort, I breakfasted at a table set with knife, fork, spoon – and binoculars, the last-named being kept handy in case an eagle swept into view. The family cat stalked cuckoos and corncrakes. There were languid conversations and throats lubricated by wee drams. If a bottle was opened, it was customary to toss the cork on to the fire, the presumption being that the whisky would be drunk before bedtime.

Delving in Ian's library of local books, I read that Rum's native population was shipped to Canada to make way for sheep farming. The island subsequently became a sporting estate, the preserve of a few rich men and their retainers, the fashion now being to shoot deer and drive grouse and to fish for salmon and trout. The second Marquis of Salisbury, who bought the island in 1845, introduced fallow deer to Rum. The experiment came to nought. He imported red deer from estates in Scotland and English parks. Nature cut the stock down to an appropriately smaller size.

Enter: John Bullough, textile manufacturer of Accrington, in Lancashire, who wanted sport and peace from the busy commercial world. He bought the island and lived in old Kinloch Lodge. He was succeeded by his son, George, who replaced the old, rat-infested Lodge with a spoof castle, an Edwardian extravaganza, with attendant Japanese garden and turtle pond. The legacy of the Bulloughs was still in everyone's mind when I first landed on the island, then known as Rhum, and when I listened to the out-of-condition Orchestrion emitting strains from Wagner. On an otherwise still night, the wheezy sounds brought several inquiring people from their beds.

Back in the Yorkshire Dales, after my first visit, invited to talk to the fifteen members Settle Rotary Club, I chose Rum as the subject. I would not be contradicted. Surely, nobody in that small, landlocked Yorkshire town would know anything about the Hebridean island. The chairman, a local baker, said he had often sailed by Rum. The father of the doctor who thanked me had visited Rum when it was The Forbidden Island and had swum in the loch. A solicitor who lived at Casterton, in the valley of the Lune, told me that his neighbour was the last of the Bulloughs, former owners of the island. At another Rotary Club, fifteen miles away, having given the same talk, I met a Rotarian whose son was studying deer on Rum.

Road To The Isles

*The road ends just beyond Mallaig and cars have to return
the same way, unless they are shipped to Skye.*
G Douglas Bolton

Several times I used the Iron Road, known prosaically as the
Mallaig Extension of the West Highland Railway. After clearing
Fort William, it ran straight and level along the lonely shoreline of
Loch Eil, haunt of shelduck, eider and wading birds. I glimpsed The
Devil's Staircase, an imposing staircase of locks that connect the
Caledonian Canal with the sea. Our little group of adventurers once
sailed down the Canal in a plastic boat to meet waves several feet high
in Loch Ness. On consulting the chart, we found only one piece of
information. Under a sketch of the Loch Ness monster was a depth
reading of nine hundred feet.

Beyond the canal outlet, the mountains closed in. I scanned the
landscape for deer, monarchs of the glens. Then the railway broke
free of tawny uplands at the head of Sheil – a sea loch in a romantic
setting. A memorial to the Jacobite Uprising sustained the romantic
theme – an exclamation mark set in stone, topped by a sculpture of
a Highlander. Glenfinnan proved to be well within the midge zone.
We once stayed at a hotel where, in the evening, we were cautioned
about the pipes. Thinking it was a reference to the plumbing, we
were ill-prepared for the appearance of a piper in full Highland dress.

Loch Sheil and its fabulous glen were seen from a height of a
hundred feet as the train clattered over Concrete Bob's gleaming
white viaduct. Robert (later Sir Robert) McAlpine, railway-builder
extraordinary, based in Glasgow, had the contract for the line to
Mallaig. His two sons, Robert and Malcolm, were involved in its day-
to-day construction. Concrete was used on a more liberal scale than

ever before for such works. The Finnan valley was spanned by a structure of twenty-one arches. Slender white pillars, rising for a hundred feet, supported arches with fifty foot spans. Concrete was mixed for other viaducts, the technique being stretched close to the limit at Borrowdale, where the bridge had a clear span of 127 ft six inches, flanked by twenty foot spans. Bob's enthusiasm for concrete extended to station buildings and, at Mallaig, to the harbour works.

The track to Mallaig had an aversion to going straight. The line had numerous tunnels and a hundred cuttings. From the train to Mallaig, I saw a narrow glen and Loch Eilt, choppy and chilly, like a sea in captivity. The river Ailort was followed to where it entered Loch Ailort, now a goodly way below the level of the line. My attention went to Loch nam Uamh – and to the open sea. Fort William, though tide-washed twice a day, was situated far from the fishing and crofting communities.

Fish was perishable stuff. When the West Highland Railway had promoted its Mallaig Extension Bill in January, 1894, it had the fisherfolk in mind. Subsequently, the trade in fish did not meet the expectations of the railway company. One reason was the Highland conscience. There must be no unnecessary work on the Sabbath. Week-end fish must wait until Monday to be sent on its way to the English market. Mallaig, the most westerly harbour on the mainland, and at one time the busiest herring port in Europe, was to adjust its activity to catching prawns and other shellfish.

Mostly, I went from Fort William to Mallaig by road. The worst hazard on the forty-seven mile stretch, then largely unimproved, was meeting an articulated fish-lorry – a fish-freezer juggernaut – on a bend or short, sharp hill. A lorry driver, in his haste to convey Hebridean herring to market on the Continent, did his best to straighten out the road. On a frosty morning, I might see a fish-lorry on its side in a ditch.

Our little group of adventurers chose the Easter week for our jaunts, during which we took on a mental age of eleven, especially when there was a burn to dam or a stone to skim across a lochan. In early spring, new growth showed through frosted vegetation in the glens and a patch of roadside daffodils contrasted with the cores of ancient snowdrifts on otherwise blue-grey hills. Red deer wore their tattered winter coats.

As the Road to the Isles enfolded, the various aspects of West Highland scenery materialised like transformation scenes in a pantomime – dazzling sea lochs and lochans in the pockets of great hills. Waterfalls tumbled from ragged glens. Birch trees, fanned by a breeze, had shivering leaves. The drab moorland would come into its own in late summer with the flowering of the ling. Shell-sand beaches of Omo-whiteness fringed the open sea.

George arranged for us to stay at the Lochailort Hotel, the interior of which was featured in a cinema film called *Local Hero*. Mine-host had a video copy of the film but a non-technical person or persons unknown had accidentally wiped it clean. Many moons ago, G Douglas Bolton, writer and photographer, stayed here on a wild September night. He dined by candlelight, drinking coffee and eating biscuits beside a peat fire. He read about Prince Charles by firelight and a flickering paraffin lamp. A guttering candle provided light as he went along panelled passages to his bedroom.

Things had improved when we visited Lochailort. As the owner, our good friend Alex Duncan, saw us draw up in the car park he arranged for the appropriate number of large drams to be set out on the edge of the bar awaiting our entry. As one who did not care for whisky, but was scared to admit it in Scottish company, I disposed of mine in a handy pot-plant. Alex asked John Broadley if he would like an oyster or two. John was partial to oysters but felt that he would not be able to afford them. Alex retired and re-appeared with a bucket of oysters, remarking to an astonished John: "Och – help yourself!"

George recalled a Friday evening at Lochailort when the bar-topics included the island of Rum, which had just come up for sale on the open market. Joining the discussion was none other than Compton Mackenzie, of *Whisky Galore* fame. He was *en route* to Canna to meet his good friend John Campbell. Invited to comment on the sale, Compton Mackenzie thought it would be in the best interest of all to pull the plug on the bloody island, as it was no good for man or beast. George told me that Arab interests were intent on buying the lot for £5 million. Nothing came of the proposal. The Nature Conservancy acquired Rum for a pittance.

Having spent a week at the hotel, with full board, including packed lunches, and with the lads running up a huge bill at the bar for the best malt whisky, we shuddered at the thought of the bill we would receive. It turned out to be £100 a head, a bargain price. George then mentioned the bar bill. Said Alex: "Forget it." We each paid our whack. As we left, the good-natured Alex felt he had overcharged us and invited us to "tak a bottle each of malt whisky – as a discount."

Another time, en route to Rum, George and I broke our journey with an overnight at the Lochailort Hotel only to be invited to dinner at the big-hoose by Mrs Cameron-Head. One of George's sons had helped out at the castle. This huge building stood in the midst of plenty. The loch was teeming with fish. Numerous cats stalked mice in the house and garden. The hills were alive with red deer. Our hostess was resplendent, from neck to ground, in tartaned Highland garb. She favoured ground-sweeping clothes because she lived in a midge-zone. Once, at Glenfinnan Games, when the wee critters were in a savage mood, she had been observed lifting a hem of her long skirt and squirting some insect repellent onto her legs.

At dinner in the big-hoose, which was also attended by a raven-haired young lady, Mrs Cameron-Head was affability itself. Her trailing garb did not reflect her social rank. This time she was "dressed for draughts". A dozen eager currents of cold air met and mingled in the vast dining room. We sat at one end of a table that seemed to stretch to infinity and were under the unblinking gaze of tartan-clad ancestors set in ornate picture frames. Carpets flapped. The wooden blocks that had formed a tight pattern on the floor of a long passage leading the toilet had now worked loose, rising and clicking back into position with every footfall. The toilet occupied a corner of a huge room.

On the way to Mallaig, I usually hummed *Road to the Isles* and snatches of *Hebrides Overture*, with its evocation of waves pounding a rocky coastline. The composer Mendelssohn and a German friend toured the Highlands in 1829. Mendelssohn wrote "it is no wonder that the Highlands have been called melancholy. But two fellows have wandered through them, laughed at every opportunity, rhymed and sketched together, growled at one another and at the world if they happened to be vexed or found nothing to eat, devoured everything in sight when they did find it and slept twelve hours a day. These two were we – and we'll not forget it as long as we live…" It was in such a spirit that three Yorkshiremen and a Scotsman – we three – approached the Hebrides.

Morar, its white-sand beach draped with cast-up weed, was best avoided when midges were in a feeding frenzy. Beyond the beach lay the sparkling sea and the Small Isles. These were just a few of the "isles of the sea", the derivation of the name Hebrides. W H Murray wrote of Atlantic islands ravaged by sea and wind. "A grey seal on a skerry might be their badge and the rain-cloud their banner."

Mallaig, where the Road to the Isles reached the sea and the West Highland Line had its railhead, sprawled across a hillside above its little harbour. At first the Iron Road to the Isles terminated at Fort William. When a port was proposed, and Loch Nevis came to mind, topographical problems led to a decision to develop remote and lightly-populated Mallaig. Donald McDonald, a critic of the plan, declared: "Mallaig is no harbour at all. It is just a pretty wee bay."

This was a work-a-day place – a community with its sleeves rolled up, evolving through the development of the herring fishery and burgeoning with the establishment of the railhead and the pier from which big boats went island-going. The harbour-side was a colourful jumble of buildings old and new. Trawlers fidgeted at their moorings as though anxious to be back at sea. Brucie Watts's boat, *The Western Isles,* was being prepared for a trip. I gave it a cheerful hand-wave, hoping Brucie would notice, and then sought the fish and chip shop, approaching the counter along a passage and rapping on a partition for attention. With the tasty fare swaddled in newsprint, I headed for the harbourside, eating the fish and chips under the gaze of herring gulls, perched at six-inch intervals along roofs and railings.

Mallaig became, for me, a place of broken sleep. Once, on a Deer Society expedition, I rejoiced that my hotel bedroom overlooked Rum and regretfully gave it up for a woman member who arrived unexpectedly. Now I had to share a bed with a Scotsman who drank whisky until well into the night – and then flopped into bed in a drunken stupor, snoring so loudly that the bedroom window rattled. A ceilidh was in progress in a wooden hut across the way. Turning-out time brought at medley of shouting, singing and car-door slamming.

Mallaig nights were never long. Bed and breakfast at one estab-lishment turned out to be a facility on a cash-down basis. We had a kick on the bottom of the bedroom door when it was time to rise to catch the early ferry sailing and, in the absence of breakfast, guzzled fresh scones at the back door of a local bakery.

Brucie's Boat

There is a great deal of stormy magnificence about the lofty
cliffs... The interior is one heap of rude mountains.
John MacCulloch, about Rum (1824)

I first crossed the Sound of Sleet from Mallaig to Rum in *The Western Isles*, owned and skippered by Bruce Watts, who made up in strength and navigational skill what he lacked in height. Brucie, as many called him, was lean, laconic and trustworthy in any sort of weather. He and his boat were veterans of the angry sea. A fellow passenger said: "We're in for a rough crossing. Brucie's got his hat on!" George Logan recalled a February morning when he strode down to the harbour at the head of a party of deer-watchers to find big waves smacking their lips against the jetty and the wind playing a 'cello solo on the telephone wires. The sky was blue-black, like Stephen's ink.

George clambered aboard *The Western Isles* and thumped a booted foot on the deck. Ere long, a tousle-haired Bruce appeared. "Are we goin' to Rum, Brucie?" asked George. Brucie looked into the blackest part of the sky, reflected for a moment or two, then said: "Och, aye. It's clearin' a bit." And off they went, with the few passengers too busy holding on to the superstructure to be sick. When the islands were served by a steamer, as opposed to diesel craft, a visitor, irritated by a delay, was told by a local man: "Och, well, she'll be coming sometimes sooner; and sometimes, maybe, she'll be coming earlier; and sometimes she'll be coming before that again."

The fishermen of the Atlantic seaboard were characters to a man. One of them accidentally hauled up the trans-Atlantic cable. His deed was noticed from the shore. In due course, he was interviewed about it. He denied touching the cable. What, then, was he handling? "Och, but it's these atomic power stations. They pump hot water into the sea. Seaweed's growing so big it's as thick as your arm." I heard the improbable tale of the island of Muck that when a wedding supper lasted many days, the whisky supply held up but they had to send to the mainland for some drinkable water.

MacBraynes ran the Small Isles Service (cafeteria facilities). It was said that –

God made the world
And all it contains;
Except the Western Isles –
And they were made by MacBraynes.

Their ferry, *Loch Arkaig*, which called at Eigg, Muck, Rum and Canna, was originally an inshore minesweeper of 179 tons, the design being based on a wooden hull so that in her quest for mines she would not detonate any of them. Launched during the Second World War, she disappointed her builders by capsizing. For service on the Small Isles run, she carried an impressive amount of iron ballast. MacBraynes, who bought her in 1959, gave her a substantial metal superstructure. She rolled in an uneasy sea. To the writer Noel Banks, "her lounge is reminiscent of a seaside-promenade shelter; only tea and buns are available."

Mr Curtis, a former chaplain of Giggleswick School who spent his main holiday in Scotland, remembered when the ferry skipper and the stationmaster were not on the best of terms. On the day when the stationmaster waved the train away minutes before the ferry docked, Mr Curtis was seen rushing up to a taxi with the words "Follow that train!"

One Easter, in the company of Fred Smart, a fellow Yorkshireman, and the indispensible George, the *Arkaig* left Mallaig promptly at 6.00 a.m. Flakes of snow glistened in the beam from the deck lights.

As daylight seeped through the clouds, we saw the hills of Skye had been whitened by snow. The *Arkaig* had no hold for goods, no covered space for cattle or sheep. An Aberdeen Angus bull had been swung aboard in a special crate, dangling from a crane, and the bull, still in its crate, would be off-loaded into a much smaller ferry off Eigg. In the early morning, a pale figure in pyjamas and dressing gown rose from a pile of lifejackets he had spread on the floor as a mattress. The figure moved haltingly to the galley for a cup of tea and then visited the toilets. He emerged washed, shaved and ready for work as the Min. Ag. Vet who was about to test the cattle of Eigg.

The *Arkaig* was under the control of jovial, rotund Willie Callander, with whom we discussed his special love – Gaelic prose and song. When he beamed, it was like having a second daybreak. George Logan was one of the passengers on the *Arkaig* when, on passing the Point of Sleet, he was surprised to see about fifty trawlers ahead. Had a large shoal of fish come into the Couillin Sound? No. Willie Callender said the boats were collecting telegraph poles that had been the deck cargo of a freighter; they had been cast overboard when it became stormbound in the Minch.

Willie had a notion that gulls were the reincarnation of old seamen, some having stripes on their wings. He was doubtless thinking of the brown marks on immature birds. After offloading the bull in its crate, also several passengers and goods, the *Arkaig* made the short crossing to Muck, where once again we were attended by an island boat. Rum was now in prospect. I went below for coffee. A corpulent member of the crew who was preparing a meal of braised steak and onions covered a dish with silver foil and remarked laconically: "It'll be all right – unless this lot flies out of the oven as we leave Muck!" The sea was kind and the food survived.

In the Sound of Rum, porpoises were hoop-la'ing against a backdrop of Askival and its retinue of mountains that were linked together by thin ridges. Manx shearwaters, the smallest, commonest of their kind, sliced the air – and occasionally the crests of waves – with their long, slim wings. When a shearwater banked, it showed the light tones of its underparts. Another flick of the wings, and the dark upper plumage was in view. I noticed that the wings, set at the centre of the bodies, completed the form of a cross. Other birds performed an aerial ballet over a distant patch of sunlit water.

One of the mountains of Rum is associated by name with trolls, the figments of Norse imagination. Trolls were small, hunch-backed, malicious creatures. They moved about at night and, if the light of day fell upon them, were turned into pillars of stone. Were the "trolls" of Rum the shearwaters, flickering and yodelling as they flew to their hilltop nesting burrows after dark?

Robert Atkinson, in his splendid book *Island Going*, described his quests for shearwaters and petrels on the remoter Scottish islands in the 1930s. The steamer that took him to the island of Eigg "ploughed flocks of shearwaters. The birds flew so low they nearly met their images in the oily calm; the set performance of flap and glide was as much a rhythm of rise and fall as telegraph wires seen from a train…"

My attention was now wholly on Rum, which is composed of igneous heaps rising to impressive domed shapes. Five of the hills of Rum have an elevation of over 2,000 ft and three of them overtop the 2,500 ft contour. The name Rum is said to be derived from the Norse word Rom, meaning wide or spacious, and Norsemen were said to have named the mountains that, occupy almost half the island. Those names – Askival, Hallival, Trollaval, Ainshval, Ruinsival – have a frosty northern sound. Perhaps the seafarers from Scandinavia, sailing their slender longboats between the Hebridean islands used the peaks of Rum as navigational aids. Little evidence exists of their actual landing on the island. The mountains were sculpted by glacial ice. Askival, the highest point at 2,659 ft., and Hallival, at 2,365 ft., are linked by a sharp ridge.

Hugh Miller, who summered in the Hebrides in 1844, his base the Free Church yacht named *Betsy*, wrote vividly of a gale and the existence of clouds on the Scurr of Eigg and the steep peaks of Rum. "Clouds seemed as if anchored, each on its own mountain-summit, and over which the gale failed to exert any propelling power. They were stationary in the middle of the rushing current, when all else was speeding before it…[In fact] instead of being stationary, they are ever-forming and ever-dissipating – clouds that form a few yards in advance of the condensing hill and that dissipate a few yards after they quit it."

In the north-eastern part of Rum, the hills have a rosy hue from sandstones and shales in conspicuous beds. Shifted a little from the horizontal by some ancient land disturbance, they gave me the impression that the landscape was about to slip beneath the sea. South of the loch, wavelets smacked their lips against a low, wooded shore. Beyond, like a backdrop for grand opera, were the mountains. Noel Banks called them "brittle peaks and rounded domes." Lavas erupted through the ancient land surface of red sandstone at a time when volcanoes flared.

Over the space of ten thousand years – a mere blink in the story of the island – Rum had developed a mantle of alpine, bog and forest vegetation – the type associated with the cool and wet Atlantic seaboard. Botanists would eagerly seek out alpine rarities like Norwegian sandwort and penny cress, also commoner plants like moss campion, cowberry and least willow. The Scottish asphodel is a much-sought-after bogland plant. Nowadays, it is enough to photo-graph, instead of pick, the astonishing plant.

The Bullough Connection

Rhum was Paradise to John Bullough. He revelled in the
sport and the restfulness the island provided.
R S Crossley (1930)

Early people flit, as insubstantial as shadows, across the early pages
of the history of Rum. In contrast, the Bulloughs have merited
several chapters to themselves. John Bullough, the first of his family
to be associated with Rum, was the son of James, who worked for a
firm of cotton manufacturers keen to make technical improvements
to weaving machinery. A restless and ambitious man, he went into
business on his own account, then into partnership with John
Howard in the running of the Globe Works at Accrington. Howard
and Bullough employed a skilled workforce to make textile
machinery, much of which was exported.

John, who was six years old when his father entered into the
partnership, was encouraged to do well by Martha, his mother, who
sent him to a college in Hampshire where Quaker teachers had
installed science into the curriculum. John advanced to the
University of Glasgow. He did not graduate, being keen to enter his
father's firm, which he enhanced through his good ideas and his
vigour. When James, his father, died in 1867, a year after his partner,
John Bullough was in charge of a thriving business employing three
hundred men. Howard and Bullough became renowned for their
ring-frames and for machinery powered by electricity. Bullough
stood out from other industrialists, who were Liberals, in being a
Conservative, a devotee of capitalism, with no room for government
interference in business.

John, aware of the adage that "all work and no play makes Jack a
dull boy", delegated responsibility to managers so that, while still

young, he could enjoy country pleasures and at the same time attain social standing as a landowner. It was the period when new-rich from the English industrial towns were colonising Scotland. John Bullough's bid came initially at Castle Meggernie, which presided over 50-square mile estate in Glen Lyon, Perthshire. Keen on scientific developments, he used the telegraph to keep in touch with his works at Accrington. A contemporary account relates that "like many other English gentlemen, he was passionately fond of shooting. His prowess as a sportsman was testified by the numerous deer and hundreds, perhaps thousands, of rabbits and hares which he sent to Accrington for sale in aid of the funds of the new Conservative Club."

John leased Rum for its sport. In 1886, having been charmed, he bought the island for £150,000. Another prospective buyer had been dissuaded by a friend's report that Rum was "difficult of access, climate abominable and everything uncomfortable. Ugh! Ugh! I wouldn't live in the place tho' you gave me it for nothing..." Lord Salisbury, the predecessor of the Bulloughs, had replaced sheep with red deer, a stock that now totalled six hundred. John brought some Royal blood into the herd, importing stags and hinds from Windsor Great Park – and doubtless letting all his friends know about it. He built lodges and instituted a programme of tree-planting at Kinloch. Then, as an amateur poet, donning the proverbial rose-coloured spectacles, he wrote:

> There's a land in the West –
> Tis the isle I love best;
> There the lordly stag doth roam
> And the eagle makes his home.

Another time, he reflected in verse his contentment with rural pleasures:

With simple wants not ill supplied,
From moor and mountain and the tide,
There comes good health and peace of mind –
The best philosophy for mankind.

John shocked his friends and business associates by divorcing his first wife, who was Alice Schmidlin, the daughter of a Swiss cotton manufacturer. They had two sons, the eldest being George, who – as Sir George Bullough – would play a dominant role in the history of the island. A second marriage, in 1885, was to Alexandra Marion McKenzie, the attractive young daughter of a Stornoway bank manager. George Bullough, feeling more than regard for his stepmother, was sent on a world cruise. It was while he was away from home, in February 1891, that John Bullough died from a lung infection while travelling to Monte Carlo.

About 1,600 people attended his funeral at Accrington. The offici-ating clergyman described him as "a master of men who made our town what it is". The local newspaper recorded that "discipline was one of Mr Bulllough's cardinal principles. Globe Works was no place for the lazy or indifferent workman." At the time of John's death, the firm of Howard and Bullough had 2,250 employees and his estate was valued at £2,500,000.

Rum became an island of romance for Sir George Bullough, a fabulously-rich Edwardian who developed it as a sporting estate, complete with a castellated shooting lodge fit for a king. Kinloch Castle, as it was grandly known, was fashioned of stone shipped from a quarry in Arran, 160 miles away. A mausoleum, styled like a Doric temple, was an incongruous feature on deer-cropped turf, against a wild Atlantic shore. Here was the final resting place of John and George Bullough, whose Hebridean reign spanned seventy years.

During that time, Rum became known as The Forbidden Island.

Derek Cooper has referred to the history of Rum as "one of the saddest and most secluded...in the Hebrides." The by-name Forbidden Island was possibly first used in the 1820s after the inhabitants were given assisted passages to Canada. (Some have compared it to an eviction). From 1847 to 1957, the title related to the exclusive use of Rum by several wealthy families. No special guard was kept on Rum but anyone landing in the hope of finding overnight accommodation was disappointed. A canoeist who slyly came ashore in the 1940s said it was "inhospitable by deliberate attempt." A Mountaineering Club, arriving unheralded in Loch Scresort by motor boat, in the summer of 1933, solved the problem of accommodation by returning to the boat at bedtime.

In the 1970s, when I visited Rum, access for the general public was restricted to day visits to the area around Loch Scresort. Only scientists, naturalists and mountaineers were allowed to stay longer on the island after obtaining permission from the Nature Conservancy. The scientist visitors to Rum made this rockscape one of the best-documented islands in Britain.

George Bullough, aged twenty-one, inherited Rum, demolished the old house where father had stayed and built a fairy-tale castle that J Morton Boyd was to describe in 1972 as "rather grand but oddly aloof mansion house." George's wife, Monica, a celebrated Edwardian beauty, lived on into her nineties and sold Rum to the Nature Conservancy in 1957 for a modest £23,000. Today, Rum is a National Nature Reserve, noted for red deer husbandry and restoration of native woodland to areas that were debased through excessive sheep-grazing. The mighty Globe Works at Accrington, after passing through several owners, closed down. The offices are now the Globe Centre.

When Rum became the property of the Nature Conservancy in 1957, it was planned to restore a sheep-degraded habitat and to study and manage the red deer. On my first visit, the schoolmistress – a Canadian – was the only person not in the employ of the Conservancy. Ian, the ferryman, was employed in various jobs, giving priority to operating the island ferryboat, *Rhouma*, between a concrete slipway and the *Arkaig*, which because of her draught could not venture as far as the shore. Ian, well-built, dark-complexioned, was at the wheel on my first visit as the island ferry approached in a flurry of white water. The rose-red castle built for Sir George Bullough stood in majesty above a line of trees – themselves a rare sight on this wild, storm-lashed Hebridean island.

A Limping Pilgrim

Remote, little sea-girt worlds, each cherishing its own wild traditions.
Edwin Waugh (1883)

The pilgrim who limped described himself thus in the title of a book that contained his memories of visiting Rum. Edwin Waugh, of Rochdale, joined a boat in the Clyde. "We steam away from Greenock about nine o'clock… I lie down on some hay in a sheltered part of the boat, looking up at the moon and listened to a highland herdsman who is crooning a wild monotonous Gaelic song, over and over again, till I fall asleep." The boat was moored at Oban for an hour and the voyage continued up the Sound of Mull. At Salem, they took aboard "thirty head of wild-looking highland cattle".

Edwin Waugh was a Rochdale man who, in a few prolific years, wrote verse for ordinary people in their own language. His word was compared with that of Robert Burns, who half a century before left a treasury of vivid works. An admirer of Waugh living in Burnley considered that he and his confreres had done for Lancashire what Burns and Hogg had done for the Scottish Lowlands – "you have immortalised a dialect and made it classical." Waugh's best poetic work had been completed by 1870. He none the less remained a notable literary figure in his native county. On his visit to Rum in 1882 he showed his mastery of prose. His impressions of the island were widely read and enjoyed when published by John Heywood in Manchester.

His charming account of life on Rum, in the John Bullough period, includes some historical information. The story of Rum as a sporting estate really began in 1845 when the Marquis of Salisbury bought the island for £24,000 and reintroduced a stock of red deer. Sheep had displaced the deer. Lord Salisbury's object was to create a sporting estate, which led him to improve the salmon and sea trout fisheries, a project that provided employment for people rendered destitute by the potato famine of 1847. He had a major plan for diverting the waters of the Kilmory River into the river flowing down Kinloch Glen. The massive stone-built dam was inadequately anchored on peaty ground. Shortly after completion, it burst. The flood scoured out Kilmory Glen. The Campbells of Ormsary purchased Rum from Salisbury in 1869. They increased Rum's value as a sporting estate until they could let it for an annual rent of £800.

The steamer on which Edwin Waugh travelled from the Clyde in 1882 departed from its usual route to put him ashore on Eigg. The captain "sets the steam-whistle going as a signal for a boat to put off from the island." The night was spent at a clean and comfortable little inn. Next day, about noon, Edwin Waugh was conveyed to Rum in an open boat. He landed on an island with few facilities and no roads "except a wandering slip of road, about half a mile long, which leads from the rude pier on the south side of Scresort Bay, through a straggling cluster of eight or ten thatched cottages called The Town."

His friendship with John Bullough meant that in his "closing years… comfort was secured by a handsome annuity" and also a home on the island of Rhum "as long as he wished to stay". He presumably had quarters at Kinloch House, also known as Tigh Mor, built early in the 19th century by a Dr Maclean some time after his brother, MacLean, the laird of Coll, had bought the island from Clanranald. The house, stone-built, with a steeply-pitched roof, took shelter from an acre of mature woodland known as The Park. Kinloch House had two small wings, one holding the gunroom and the other the kitchen. In the absence of a glazier, if a pane in a bedroom window was broken, the fractured part was overlaid with another piece, "which serves at least to keep out the wind, although it slightly dims the light."

Hard by Kinloch House was the dwelling house and farmstead of Donald Ferguson, sheep farmer. The rest of the buildings at Kinloch were "mere Highland huts. Waugh was told that three or four families, living elsewhere, might be found "in solitary nooks of the isle, such as the lonely hollow of Papadala, with its little loch; the wild glen of Harris; and the pastoral dell of Kilmory." The Rev John Sinclair made periodic visits from Eigg and officiated at a tiny chapel furnished by a small deal table and a few wooden forms. On a fine Sunday, there would be over twenty worshippers – not forgetting the sheepdogs which, having followed their masters, lay about on the floor or under the forms or "go lazily in and out at the open door…" At ordinary times, the service was in Gaelic; but if any visitors happened to be present the service would be followed by a short act of worship in English.

Waugh witnessed an interment in the old graveyard and noted: "There was neither bell, book, nor candle used when the remains of old Malcolm were laid down in Kilmory; where generation after generation of the inhabitants of the Isle of Rum have been buried during the last thousand years. The soil of that lonely weed-grown God's Acre is thick with mouldering relics of the wild forefathers of the island; and when the body of the 'old captain' was brought by his neighbours to mingle with the rest in this last gathering ground of mortal decay, no prayers were said, no funeral rites were observed, nor was there a word spoken by the simple shepherds and fishers who had brought him there. Yet although they "carved not a line, nor raised a stone', to mark his resting place, they seemed to have thought that it would be all the better for a little sculptured covering of some sort, so they took an old time-worn stone with an inscription upon it which was almost undecipherable, and saying amongst themselves, 'Oh, this 'll do!' they quietly laid it upon the old man's new-made grave, and then came away, leaving the tenants of the silent land to 'sort themselves'."

After old Malcolm's death, his aged sister, Mary, took possession of the forty shillings he had left, and of his cottage, with all that was therein; "And there she lives now, all alone, waiting for the coming hour when the neighbours will have to carry her also across the hills, or round the shore in a boat, to the old graveyard at Kilmory."

Visiting sportsmen who stayed at Kinloch House set out in the morning, "clad in their shooting gear, with their guns and their gillies, and their deer-stalkers and their dogs bounding around them, wild with delight." If the sportsmen lingered on the hills long after night had fallen, guns were fired off at the rear of the house. "Sometimes this brought a signal shot in reply from the returning sportsmen, far away up the dark glen."

One time, two of the men returned, sodden and "half covered with peat mire", to report that the pony – which was carrying a slain stag – was fast in a bog nearly five miles away. The two men had some refreshment, then set off with lanterns and ropes. The pony was released in such an exhausted state it could not stand. "After pouring a bottle of whisky down its throat they laid a quantity of oatcake near its head and then left it there to live or die, as the case might be." It was the last we heard of it.

First Impressions

Bad roads. Peats ditto. Lochs inaccessible... No salmon...
Climate abominable.
Andrew Forester, writing to J A Harvie-Brown (1886)

*L*och *Arkaig* departed at speed. Standing at the head of the slipway on Rum, above an area of green slime and washed-up kelp, Fred, George and I listened to the crooning of eiders. Hooded crows were rooting among the kelp littering the shore. One crow rose with a mussel and dropped it, intent on cracking the shell on rock. Robert Buchanan, a Victorian visitor, in his seven-ton yacht *Tern*, described the hooded crow as "monstrous". He saw the bird at the northern point of Loch Scresort, where "gulls innumerable sit and bask." The crow uttered its croak as it "perched like an evil spirit on the very head of the cliffs... squinting fiercely at the far-off sheep."

Buchanan, on his visit to Rum in 1872, saw a "rude stone pier... off which a battered old brigantine is even now unloading oatmeal and flour." He rowed over to the vessel for a chat with "the shrewd-looking ancient skipper". The skipper spoke in "that extraordinary dialect called Gaelic-English, which may be described as a wild mingling of Gaelic, bad Irish and lowland Scotch". He cruised from island to island in summer, bartering his cargo of food for "whatever marketable commodities the poor folk of the place may have prepared."

George remembered when a Clyde "puffer", named *Raylight*, arrived with a cargo of coal. It appeared in the early hours, at high tide, and grounded at the pier for the unloading operation by all-hands, which must be completed before the boat floated off at the next high tide. Subsequently, as the *Raylight* was taking a load of explosives to Northern Ireland, there was an accidental explosion and the "puffer" was lost, with what loss of life George had not discovered.

Rum also had an annual visit from a Glasgow dentist who spent his holidays visiting the Small Isles. His yacht was kitted out as a dentist's surgery and on his visit to Rum the staff and children were examined and any necessary work undertaken. The children of Ian and Cath hated to see the dentist arrive but attendance was compulsory. The dentist's visits ceased when the wife of a new member of the staff, being a dentist, established a surgery at the castle.

Now I was on an island where most of the effort went into studying the footloose red deer. It was Sir Frank Fraser Darling, who at a time when much research was undertaken in musty laboratories, opened the windows to outdoor study and remarked that Rum should be seen as "a natural laboratory." The only time I saw him was at the annual meeting of the British Deer Society in Perth. We were at adjacent tables. I was tongue-tied in the presence of an august naturalist. He turned to me and said: "May I parasitise you?" He wanted to borrow the sugar basin.

A red stag, with a lusty growth of new horn, hung about a few hundred yards from the houses of Kinloch as though waiting patiently for dusk, when it might raid the gardens. The folk of Kinloch accepted deer as part of the scene, to the extent that they no longer really noticed them. Yet telegraph poles had been wrapped around with barbed wire so that deer would not be tempted to rub against them.

Venison was hanging in an outbuilding designated as a larder. Nearby, in a railed-off plot, deer bones were strewn to be cleansed by insects prior to being studied. A few antlers testified to the fitness of the stags but most of the antlers had been left on the hill, to be chewed up – recycled, indeed – so the stags that were growing new antlers could re-absorb some of the calcium they contained. Pregnant hinds were attracted to cast antlers.

Ian Simpson, having secured the island ferryboat, directed me to the post office, which was presided over by his wife Kathy. We elected to walk to Ian's house. Our route lay through a tract of spring-fresh woodland. We crossed a bridge spanning the Kinloch River and paused to admire Rum ponies grazing on a hillside. An unlikely tale claimed that the ponies were descended from stock that swam ashore from a wrecked galleon of the Spanish Armada. These had been introduced from Erinskay.

The fearsome-looking Highland cattle, which I first got to know as an illustration on the wrappers of Holland's toffee, are gentle – most of the time. When, in 1971, it was decided to introduce a small herd to Rum they took a dislike to the craft allocated for the job – it was the Knoydart Estate's landing craft, *Spanish John* – and, breaking free, led their drovers on a merry round of the streets of Mallaig. I was advised not to try to pat or stroke them!

Ian, Cath and their children had a detached house with a view of Lock Scresort from the living room – an essential feature for a ferryman. The main item on the menu was venison from deer culled from the herd. I had never consumed such a large quantity of this rich, lean meat. Cath had considerable experience of preparing venison for the table but after several meals, my digestive system was sluggish and it was a delight to sample ham and local eggs. The owner of Rum, in 1828, had followed the latest craze in the Highlands, shipping the islanders to America and bringing in a few shepherds and 8,000 sheep, but the last of the sheep had been shot off. Red deer once again had a monopoly.

With the radio used only for a daily news programme and the weather forecasts, and no television, Ian had a vast library of Hebridean books. Visitors to his home meant fresh talk and so in the late evening, with the young folk in bed, a bottle of whisky was uncorked – and wee drams were in order. Whisky, the "water of life", was regarded by the islanders as a medicine for "ye canna manish wi'oot it." I was told of a Highland inn where a garden wall was formed of empty whisky bottles that had been cemented together. One windy night, the blast whistled and wailed among the bottle necks to such effect that next day the landlord had them plugged.

Tales were told of olden time. I heard of the Scottish lady who was dying. A piper was brought in to play a lament. He did not play very well. When it was over, the bedfast lady wearily remarked: "Thank God there was nae smell." George Logan, having taken a very hot bath, opened the window to let some steam out. He left the lights burning so as not to overload the circuit. In the morning, Cath scolded him and pointed to about two inches of dead midges below the lamp. The bath and the floor were also smothered in midges.

Corncrakes nested nearby. At last light, in the nesting season, the cock bird might be seen walking round the end of the house and down the path, stopping now and again to raise its head and utter its rasping, disyllabic call – *crex, crex*. I was told it called mainly at night but I slept hard and awoke at dawn to a real-life cuckoo clock. The bird – another species with a double-note call – was perched on the garden fence no more than a hundred yards from my bedroom window. Ian's cat had stalked the cuckoo, which flew off minus one or two tail feathers.

In the early days of the Conservancy's ownership, George MacNaughton was the busiest man on the island. He was among other duties policeman, registrar, coastguard and receiver of wrecks and the Conservancy's chief emissary. He rarely disturbed those stags and hinds that grazed near the castle. One bold stag developed the bad habit of butting a person in the backside. One of the stalkers, left his bothy in the evening to relieve himself having drunk a considerable amount of canned beer. He was butted and decided that next morning the deer would "get the bullet". George Logan offered to cure the stag of its bad habit. He scooped out the centres of potatoes and filled them with mustard. When called, the stag came for the spuds. As he ate them, his eyes began to water and he shot off over the beach. The stag was not seen near the castle until the following year.

Sir George's Dream House

*Kinloch Castle on Rum, an island within an island, should be
preserved in its entirety.*
John Betjeman

To Sir George Bullough, the island was called Rhum, with an
aitch, and so it was at the time of my first visit. Newspapermen
were delighted to call it The Forbidden Island. Articles gave the
impression that strangers who landed here unannounced might be
shot on sight. Hardly. Being a private island, it did not have touristy
facilities, such as bed-and-breakfast establishments. Kinloch Castle,
which was multi-bedroomed, was for the exclusive use of family,
friends and their attendants during the shooting season. A hoary tale
related that Lady Bullough, confronting campers who had pitched
their tents on the castle lawn, ordered them off. They observed that
God, not the Bulloughs, had made Rum. She replied: "Perhaps – but
God doesn't pay the rates and taxes."

George Bullough employed Leeming & Leeming, of Victoria
Street, London, a notable firm of architects, to design his hunting
lodge on a grand scale that would replace the old, rat-infested
Kinloch House. The work was put in hand in 1897 and completed
three years later. The original design was for a hollow square, each
side being symbolically as long as Sir George's beloved steam-yacht,
the *Rhouma*. The plan was modified when there was not sufficient
room on the site, between two burns, but the result was spectacular.

There arose a two-storey mock-castle, complete with tower, corner
turrets and a covered colonnade. It was adorned by the family crest –
bullocks' heads. The three hundred-strong labour force was recruited
on Eigg and in Lancashire. Each man who agreed to wear the new
Rum tartan kilt was paid an extra shilling a week. Kilted men must

have suffered grievously from insect bites. As one of the bluff Lancashiremen remarked: "If it in't midges, it's clegs. If it in't clegs, it's rain."

John Betjeman loved this Edwardian tycoon's extravaganza, which in 1901 cost £250,000. Betjeman wrote: "The fittings and furnishings… are their own brochure and can show the whole world how a small rich part of it lived in an age which has gone for ever." Sir George had not fancied the hue of local sandstone so – as mentioned – a brighter type was shipped in from the isle of Arran. Good quality topsoil for the grounds was transported from Ayrshire. A small army of workmen planted 80,000 trees of 120 species, created rose garden and Italian garden, rockeries, fountains and glasshouses.

Sir George, Highland laird, greatly improved the sporting facilities and introduced a flock of wild goats from Perthshire, augmented in due course by some goats from the Sunart district of Argyll. The gardens were kept trim by a staff of fourteen. Grapes, peaches and nectarines were grown under glass. Six domed palm houses were the resort of humming birds. Turtles and even alligators swam in heated tanks. What better than some turtle soup after a day spent on the hills? When the work was done, and when George Bullough, his high-born wife and friends were in residence, the Scottishness of the place was accentuated when a piper played from the top of the tower at sunset.

On my first visit to Kinloch Castle, I was surprised by the modest size of the entrance hall and amused to see coat-hooks fashioned from the tines of red deer antlers. Beyond the lobby lay the glory of a galleried hall, complete with a balcony festooned with the mounted heads of stags. A concert grand – Steinway, of course – was said to be one of the best pianos of that make in Scotland. Light filtered into the hall through stained glass and the fronds of potted ferns to reveal nine foot high Japanese vases and other ornaments – a haul of expensive souvenirs that the laird and his wife had collected on world travels in their steam yacht *Rhouma*. Skin rugs, prepared from animals shot by the Master of Rum, lay about the floor.

The images of Sir George and Lady Bullough, formerly Monica, daughter of the 4th Marquis de la Pasture, were flatteringly shown on enormous oil paintings. The subjects were acquainted with the glittering social set that orbited Edward VII. When George met Monica she was a divorcee. This state did not deter John Sinclair, Minister of the Small Isles, when he was asked to conduct their marriage ceremony. It took place, amid much pomp, at Kinloch Castle, on 24 June, 1903. Lady Monica was allotted her own drawing room, in which panelled walls were inlaid with flowered silk. The furnishings were of uniform pink and white. From a white moulded ceiling were suspended lustred chandeliers.

As noted, George Logan introduced me to the Orchestrion, a product of Imhof & Mukle of Baden, who built only two of this type, the other being made for Prince Albert. Soon after the property came to the Nature Conservancy, George McNaughton had asked Ian Simpson and George Logan if they could "fettle" the Orchestrion so that it would be in good order when a Conservancy big-wig visited the island. The working was stripped and re-assembled. The instrument operated in a fashion. George supplied a new leather belt but noticed on his next visit it remained to be fitted.

Kinloch Castle was the second place in Scotland to be lit by electricity (the first was – Glasgow!). The current came from a hydro-electric system, activated by water that flowed through a cast-iron pipe from a small dam on the hillside. Electricity reached the house through underground cables. In the billiards room were leather armchairs and velvet curtains. Hanging from the ballroom ceiling was a huge cut-glass chandelier. I browsed in a library, its shelves stacked with about two thousand books. The ballroom was complete with a minstrel gallery. Everywhere, in this expensive folly, I saw examples of woodwork – staircases, balustrades, furnishings – created by the skill of master-craftsmen.

A stuffed eagle stared unblinkingly from a tall case. The bird's wings were partly open. One of the bird's feet rested on the body of a white mountain hare. Space in a turret room was almost fully occupied by a three-ton Asian eagle fashioned in solid bronze. Stuffed fish were from specimens from the tropics that the Bulloughs' caught during world-wide cruises in *Rhouma*, their 300 ton, twin-screw yacht. The mounted specimens included what remained of a huge fish that had been hooked, then had its tail bitten off by a shark. Not the least interesting collection were the photographs taken when the Bulloughs sailed round the world. When their yacht lay at anchor in Loch Scresort, a football team composed of members of the crew would compete with one of the island teams.

Sir George, up-to-date in his ideas, installed a ten-line telephone system – the first of its kind to be fitted to a Scottish private house. A bathroom contained what must have been a wonder of the age – a bath-cum-shower, encased in the best mahogany. I saw what looked like a combination of huge bath with a sentry box at one end. A glance behind the wooden facings of this grand structure was described by a writer in *The Scots Magazine* as "a Spaghetti Junction of lead piping taking hot and cold water from mixing valves to a series of sprays, showers, squirts and all sorts of perforated pipes." These enabled the bather to choose plunge, jet, douche or wave spray, ideal for anyone with with a bath-time duck or boat.

Visiting his castle on Rum, in what was to become known as the Edwardian Sunset, soon to end with the Great War, Sir George would be content. The third generation of the triumphant Bulloughs and an Old Harrovian, he had been given a menial job at the Globe Works to acquaint him with the source of the family wealth. His father's death rid him of the need for manual work. He was proud of a knighthood awarded in 1901, the time of the Boer War, for providing, fitting out and staffing his yacht as a hospital ship, stationed off Cape Town, ready to receive injured soldiers.

On the mainland, he officiated as a captain in the Scottish Horse and as Master of the Ledbury Hounds. He had a house in London and, being passionately fond of horse-racing, bought a mansion near Newmarket. Sir George owned a string of horses and was for seventeen years a member of the Jockey Club. Sir George and Lady Bullough stayed on Rum for about six weeks in August and September. Tweed-clad, moustached, be-capped, with tobacco pipe in mouth and stick in hand, he often took to the hills.

Lady Bullough preferred less energetic pursuits, such as golf. It was her delight to have afternoon tea served on the terrace in the company of a friend or important visitor. One guest accidentally dropped a sandwich on to the grass. He bent to pick it up but was restrained by Lady Monica, who rang for the butler, whose attention was drawn to the sandwich. The ladies talked while he returned indoors, to reappear carrying a silver salver and a pair of silver tongs. He retrieved the sandwich and placed it back on the tray. Lady Monica said to the butler: "Don't waste it. Have it for your tea."

The Bulloughs brought their house staff with them. Apart from the sandwich-recovering butler, there was a footman, valet and lady's maid. A quartet of kitchen staff ensured they were well fed. Most accounts indicated that her Ladyship was an affable if forceful person. Her husband had the ideas, and paid the bills, but it was usually she who gave the orders. In winter, when the laird and his wife were in their winter home, in the South, the factor took command at Rum. Archie Cameron, the son of one of Sir George's staff, recalled some testy factors. He also remembered that the diet was based on venison, the toughest being left to soak all night before being put in a stew-pot with swedes.

For a decade, the Bulloughs visited the island for a few weeks each year. Their regular visits ended with the outbreak of war in 1914. Sir George saw service in the Army, with the rank of Major. His beloved steam yacht, *Rhouma II*, was affiliated to the Royal Navy. The notion of Rum as The Forbidden Island was sustained when the MacBrayne ferry service delivered to the island only those who had permission to visit the place. Yet the Bulloughs seem to have been hospitable to the few folk who arrived without notice and impinged on their privacy. In later times, the forbidden state was a challenge to adventurous young people, who landed in quiet places and departed without being detected. By this time the great days of Rum as a sporting estate were over.

Kinloch Castle, Rum
Hebridean home of an Edwardian tycoon.

Left:
Fine detail of the head of a bronze eagle that was collected by Sir George Bullough on a world cruise in his steam-yacht.

Right:
George Logan, in the library at Kinloch Castle. He is glacing through one of many photograph albums recalling visits to distant lands.

Right:
Mallaig, the fishing port from which our adventures to the Small Isles began – at first in the "Western Isles," skipper Brucie Watts.

Below:
George Logan (left) with the ferrymen of Eigg, who operated twixt the main ferry and the island. They received people, goods and livestock.

Eigg, backed by the mountains of Rum, photographed from the *Arkaig*.

The Lodge on the island of Eigg.

Ian Simpson, ferryman on Rum, meets the *Arkaig* in Loch Scresort.

George Logan examines a cast red deer antler on Rum.

Great Hall of Kinloch Castle
A cover protects the Steinway piano.

An approach to the island of Canna, which had the only jetty in the Small Isles.

Tilework from the original Bullough Mausoleum. It went out of favour and was replaced by one in the style of a Grecian temple.

Loch Scresort, Rum
A safe anchorage on an otherwise inhospitable shore.

Murderous Hordes

All visitors to the Reserve in summer are vividly impressed by the abundance and vigour of the island's clegs, midges and sheep-ticks.
Dr W J Eggeling

When, during a visit by the British Deer Society, George Logan and his wife were allocated a bedroom at the rear of the castle, they left a window open and the light switched on as they went for the evening meal. On their return, they found an uncountable horde of midges had taken over. George swept them up with a vacuum cleaner. Outdoors, humans had no defence against midges save a rapid retreat for cover. From its larval stage deep in a bog, the midge emerged in summer to fly in most kinds of weather. Swat one midge and a thousand would attend its funeral. I used various anti-midge creams and lotions, also after-shave and whisky. A doctor who heard of the whisky treatment tut-tutted at the waste and added: "Are you trying to drown it?"

Edwin Waugh, the friend of John Bullough who spent several weeks on Rum during the midge season wrote that the vindictive insects descended "in murderous hordes upon every exposed bit of skin about you." In olden time a man convicted of a serious crime had been "stripped naked and tied to a stake and left exposed in the sun... till he was stung to death by the gnats and flies." Archie Cameron, who was reared on the island, described Rum midges as "indomitable, insatiable and fierce." They were, he added, the Supremos of the midge world. "I should know because I have been the basic diet for millions of them."

E M Nicholson, a Director General of the Nature Conservancy wrote: "Non-scientific visitors are often most impressed by the numbers and viciousness of the horse flies or clegs, the midges and the sheep-ticks." Campbell Steven, writing in 1955, mentioned the clegs that "descended on us in their hundred, suicidal in their thirst for human blood… Never in our lives had we experienced mass attacks like these." It was the sheep-tick I most feared. Since the sheep had been removed from Rum, deer, goats and occasion humans were the chosen prey. A tick sprang from coarse vegetation on to the legs of some luckless person or animal brushing against it.

After a day on the hills, I would scan my legs, between stockings and breeks, for specks of black – a lean tick, ready to have the meal of its life, at my expense. If left, the tick would become so bloated with blood it resembled a black grape. During the night, feeling an itch, I would rub one leg against another, then doze off, unaware that I had rubbed off the body of the tick. It had left its wicked little head in the wound and this might turn septic.

Hardy souls who found ticks upon them tickled them with the lighted end of a cigarette.

On The Tops

*Rhum is a strange place, eerie and haunted... It is all
mountain – hills as dark and savage as the Cuillins
themselves and falling for the most part steeply to the sea...*
Gavin (Ring of Bright Water) Maxwell

From a window at the ferryman's house, we scanned the loch and
focussed on a pair of red-throated divers. They swam low in the
water, like grey submarines, before diving for food. When they flew,
together, they gained height with swan-like ponderousness, banked
and were lost to sight against the dark hills. The divers would nest on
one of the freshwater lochans and dine on fish in the sea.

We sampled the weather. Rum has mild winters, with cool and
cloudy summers. John MacCulloch (1824) wrote: "If it is not always
bad weather in Rum, it cannot be good very often." Kinloch, being
on the wettest side of the Scottish islands, was momentarily dry. The
sea gleamed but it was too bright, too early – or glisky, as we call it
in my native Yorkshire Dales.

We were about to experience a typical Hebridean springtime
cocktail. Askival, the nearest of the big hills, was capped with fresh
snow. At lower level, rain turned to hail, beating a tattoo on the
window panes. Two-inch shivers beset even the Rum ponies. The air
became "close". A flash of lightning was followed by a thunderclap.
Minutes later, the world was sunny again. The radio weather forecast
mentioned the imminence of a Force 9 gale.

George, Fred and I attained the main ridge, climbing steeply from
Kinloch, scrambling on to Hallival and then venturing on to Askival,
the highspot. Another day, exploring the western hills in mist and
rain, we ate our sandwiches at 1,500 ft and marvelled at the speed
with which herring gulls converged to share the feast. Rum was

otherwise a quiet island. The honk of a hooded crow and the golden plover's sad whistle accentuated the overall quietness. The plover were nesting high on Fiunchro where heatherland gave way to grass kept fine by grazing deer, judging by copious droppings. A steep slope, bedecked by orchids, led to a flat summit, about the size of two tennis courts, where we found a welcome calm after the turbulence in the glens. Bumble bees flew sorties in thin sunlight. In summer, the islands hum with bees.

The Simpson family were never short of company. The Missionary of the Small Isles spent a day or so here. He told me of a wise-man living in Ross-shire who forecast a time when summer would be winter and winter would be summer. Brrr! A relative, who fancied himself as a piper, strode up and down at break of day filling the air with terrible sounds – until someone threatened to stuff the pipes with polyfilla.

I was to discover a brighter side to life on Rum. When the rain stopped and the cuillins had lost their bonnets of cloud; when the burn's roar became a murmur and sunlight warmed the sodden ground, the island could be enchanting, though in general terms it was a dour island, wearing dull tones. On the wild Atlantic coast were fearsome cliffs, some greatly eroded, culminating in the near-vertical Bloodstone Hill, where even the native red deer were apt to loose their footing. I saw the decaying body of a stag draped over a shrub on one of the ledges. It was during a cliff-top walk with George Logan that, during a rest for food and a nap, I slipped some chuckies [stones] into his rucksack to slow him down.

There are stones – and stones. George recounted a visit to Bloodstone beach, seeking tide-polished bloodstone and agates. At low tide he walked under a natural rock arch and a sea tunnel, forgetful of the tide which had turned as he returned. Before he reached the dry part of the beach he had waded chest-deep in the sea.

He dried out in sunlight as he slogged up the track that led back to Kinloch with a considerable load of stones.

Then it was more cliffs, more goats, in the unknown quarter of Rum where eagles played hide and seek in the mist and some of the best seabird colonies were found. It was in this area that George Logan, having run out of water, was told to rest by the indefatigable George MacNaughton, who subsequently presented him with cloudberries, alpine berries like miniature strawberries, that filled half a deer stalker's bonnet. "They were delicious."

Flowing into the sea on the south-east of Rum was a powerful river, its setting the stern glen of Dibidil. This was the wettest side of the island. Over 200 inches of teeming, tippling precipitation were expected annually. Arriving in Dibidil soaked and chilled after the long walk from Kinloch, I waded recklessly through the river and made for a modest stone building that would shelter me as I ate my sodden sandwiches. In a dream-like situation I found the building held two attractive young ladies who had just heated up some soup on a primus stove. They shared the soup with me!

Hallival was the first choice because George, who had climbed the hill umpteen times, had never stood on a feature he could see from Ian's house. It was splinter of rock jutting from an upper slope. He was determined to find that rock – and to climb it. Our path began through woodland at the back of the castle, thence through a gate in a deer fence to the open hill. On my first visit I had been introduced to several tame deer kept in an enclosure with a woodland setting. One was a hummel – a hornless stag – with which George played some circus tricks.

We rested by water so sterile it took on the green shade of the rocks beneath. Glancing at the snow-capped Cuillins of Skye, to the north, George again dipped a cupped hand into the water, drank, and remarked: "Once you start drinking ye canna stop. It's braw water."

He also testified it was cold, having slipped into the burn.

Our path ran alongside a ravine and then into a corrie, from which we viewed the Green Hill, away to the west. It was so named through being grassed over and was, said George, a favourite grazing area for deer.

We left the heather and the sound of flowing water to enter the desertland of the montane area where pipits and a golden plover tried to infuse a sense of life. Our feet were on poor, bare earth, frost-shattered rock, then on heathery land that suited that tenaciously-rooted plant called clubmoss. Soon the hilltop was shrouded in a clammy mist in which the gruff voices of ravens were heard. At the edge of a cliff, we saw a golden eagle break through the mist and glide fifty feet below us, moving slowly, silently, out of sight. The sea *har* was dangerous. George said he had seen the high slopes of Allival lightly covered with foam blown in from the Atlantic.

Rum was described by an early tourist as "the wildest and most repulsive of the islands… I tramped across the island in all kinds of weather, passing through a succession of solitudes. Yet traces can be found of the days when there was a high native population. Here and there, the ridges associated with *lazybeds* attested to the time when potatoes and cereal crops were grown. The people used seaweed as a fertiliser. On higher ground were the remnants of shielings, primitive shelters, used in summer, when women and children took domestic stock – black cattle, goat-like sheep – to the hills. Doubtless, the goodness of milk produced from a flush of new growth was locked up as cheese, to be consumed in winter.

Sheep farming robbed the island of its plentiful heather, which was replaced by bent and blue moor grass. On my first visit, Rum had experienced a long dry spell. Even so, while exploring the hinterland, boots went deeply into the expanse of sphagnum moss and peat. A hooded crow had a "larder", as evidenced by a collection of shattered eggs of other birds, plus a bird skeleton. The fact that red-throated divers were nesting near one of the lochans was borne out by the *kok-kok-kok* as a bird took flight, rising with powerful wingbeats before descending to the sea in a shallow glide. Ian told me that when standing by Loch Scresort he heard wind strumming the partly-opened wings of a diver descending to the sea to feed on fish.

Dr Johnson, in his tour of the Hebrides, saw Rum ponies which he described as being "very small but of a breed eminent in beauty." Red deer were re-introduced, the native stock having failed at the time when sheep became numerous. The *Old Statistical Account* for 1796 associated the decline of the deer with the felling of woodland in which the animals had sheltered. "While the wood throve, the deer also throve; now that the wood is totally destroyed, the deer are extirpated."

The feral goats of Rum were mentioned by Pennant, a visitor in the eighteenth century, though mainland goats, introduced in the reign of the Bullough family might have augmented the old stock. As mentioned, Highland cattle were descended from animals conveyed to Rum from Mallaig by landing-craft.

The summit of Hallival looked lifeless, yet in burrows under my feet hundreds of Manx shearwaters were sitting on eggs at the start of a protracted nesting season. They were a mile from the sea. The Manx shearwater, so named because it was first studied on the Isle of Man, is pigeon-sized with a thirty-inch wing span. It is dark grey above, white beneath, having a tubular bill and about its body a faint musty odour.

The shearwater commutes across the Atlantic to nest on the western seaboard of Europe and then returns, wintering off the coast of South America. Placing light alloy rings on the feet of shearwaters in burrows on Rum had indicated that birds of the year might be in Brazilian waters a few weeks after leaving their nests on the Hebrides.

The droppings of seabirds fertilised the ground, giving it a lush greenness that was maintained by being cropped by red deer, which in summer go high to avoid the irritation of blood-sucking insects. It was an eerie experience to be on Hallival on a moonless night as shearwaters exchanged duties. Birds that had been feeding – some of them as far south as the Bay of Biscay – returned, circling with yodelling calls before pitching down near their burrows. Someone compared the crooning and cackling sounds with those heard at an over-crowded chicken run.

The shearwaters flew by night because then their main enemies, the big gulls, were roosting. Golden eagles preyed on the birds, either striking them at first light or when there was a moon. How each bird located its nesting hole among so many, in circumstances that to me were confusing, I do not know. Could it be a distinctive scent? Or a finely-tuned sense of direction? One landed with a thump near me. Robert Atkinson, shearwatering on Eigg in 1937, saw birds that became bunkered in fern. One landed in a honeysuckle bush. "It half-opened its wings and used them like arms to clamber towards a burrow entrance higher up. When we came back in daylight and took out the heavy obstreperous young one from the first burrow, it worked its wings in just the same way and used its beak like a grappling hook to hoist itself uphill."

While one of a pair remains in the burrow, sitting a single egg, the other goes off to feed, its range extending over hundreds of miles. Then the changeover takes place. One hears the swish of wings, the yodelling calls of the birds in flight and responsive chirping from the burrows.

When the young have laid on fat from food provided by the shuttle service of their parents, they are forsaken, left to waddle, flutter or tumble down steep slopes for about 1,500 ft before reaching an unfriendly seashore. It has been known for helpless birds to be attracted by lights at Kinloch, where they were rescued from cats and kept overnight by friendly villagers, to be released into the loch on the following day. A scientist using a mercury-vapour lamp on the Castle lawn had to discontinue his moth-catching routine when the lamp attracted more than a hundred shearwaters.

George did climb his mystery rock. Anyone who ventured on to Hallival in his company was photographed in a death-defying situation, this being a rock wedged across a gorge that looked to be a thousand feet deep but was in fact less than twenty feet. The trick was to hold the camera at such an angle that only the distant background was shown.

I ascended Creag nan Stearnain (alias Bloodstone Hill) and had the wretched experience of eating tomato sandwiches in a rainstorm. I then stood at the rim of the Rgor Mhor cliffs, which descend a sheer thousand feet into the sea. Bloodstone, classified as semi-precious, is a cryptocrystaline quartz with a green stain and specks of blood-red from iron oxide, said to represent the blood shed by Christ. To early settlers, hunters then farmers, huddling in their simple shelters of wood and animal skins, it was the hardest available material, suitable for making into implements and, in the case of a Neolithic arrow-head, discovered in 1983, a weapon.

Another day I joined a small group who spent a day crossing the island from east to west – from the Scresort beach of shingle and weed to a beach in the shadow of imposing cliffs. Here, at low tide, it was safe to walk under a natural rock arch and attain the shoreline below Bloodstone Hill. Mined in Victorian times, presumably by the islanders, bloodstone was used for the seals on watch chains worn by gentlemen.

Generally, the pieces of bloodstone were small but a friend who, with his two small sons, made his precarious way along an overgrown miners' trod that was little more than a sheep-trod was discouraged by the slippery nature of the path from returning by the same route. They descended, with much anguish, and the use of a rope, one of the steep gills. He located bloodstone as big as a football but wisely decided to concentrate entirely on the rigorous descent to the shore. George had heard that a huge slab of bloodstone had been used as a table-top for a piece of furniture that came into the possession of Queen Victoria.

George had warned me about collecting too many geological specimens from the beach – not because it would have been an offence to the environment but because there would be a long slog on the return. The pathside leading back to Kinloch was littered with the fragments of jettisoned rock.

A Song Of Rum

Compiled by visiting archaeologists. To be sung to the strains of My Favourite Things from The Sound of Music.

Red deer and ponies and tractors that rattle;
NCC wardens and black Highland cattle;
Black and white sea birds that come here to nest –
These are the things about Rum we love best.

Chorus:
When the clegs bite
When the wind blows
When you want to curse –
We simply remember what we're here to do
And that makes us feel much worse.

When we're digging or wet-sieving
And we're feeling numb
Despite all the weather
We've had since we came –
We all like it here on Rum!

Verse 2
Looking for bloodstone we find entertaining:
Waking each morning to see that it's raining –
Mud in your wellies and soil in your vest,
These are the things about Rum we like best.

Chorus

Verse 3
Watching sea eagles that soar over ridges,
Looking for benchmarks that should be on bridges;
Dreaming of midges that give you no rest –
These are the things about Rum we love best.

Chorus

Verse 4
Wild goats in sea caves that frighten the walkers;
Land Rovers packed to the gunnels with stalkers,
All here to look at red deer at their best –
These are the things about Rum we love best.

Chorus

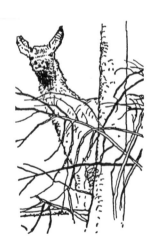

Kilmory Glen

*The largest settlement would seem to have been at Kilmory
where... as the name itself suggests, was a religious house,
with a place of burial adjacent thereto.*
Alasdair Alpin MacGregor (1953)

A broad Glen, scoured by a rush of water when a dam burst, had a
river that emptied its waters into a sandy bay on the north coast
of Rum. The heather and peat, a resort of red grouse, gave way to
dune, machair and marsh. A local guide informed me that in summer
the maritime grasslands become yellow with trefoils and hawkweeds
and purple with wild thyme, with violas and gentians. Podgy
shelduck, having hatched out their young in burrows, lead them to
water. As they process, keeping close to the parent bird, their striped
plumage resembles old-fashioned humbugs.

The Cuillins of Skye provides an astonishing backdrop. Red deer,
some with collars, to distinguish one from other, might be seen
walking along the sands. One I saw had some old fishing net entangled in its antlers. Kilmory is where the red deer were to be recorded
as never before. A long-term study of them began in 1972 under Dr
Tim Clutton-Brock and Fiona Guinness. Their quarters were in a
single-storey dwelling with a typical Scottish appearance – two ee's
[eyes – windows] and a moo' [mouth – door].

Also at Kilmory were the remains of an abandoned village –
complete with graveyard. The location of the Church of Mary from
which the name Kilmory was drawn, is not known. The one legible
memorial stone was associated with a shepherd called Murdo
Mathieson who, in 1873, mourned five of his family. They died,
victims of diphtheria, in the space of three days. Murdo emigrated
with what remained of his family to New Zealand, where he

prospered.

The laundry, built of corrugated iron, was situated at Kilmory, seven miles away (and well out of sight) of the castle. It was also in an area where drying clothes was a better proposition than at Kinloch, in the lee of the mountains. The laundry was staffed by two young maids, who hung out the washed clothes and sheets in an area known as Kilmory Greens and had them ready for collection, weekly, by a young man using a pony and cart. Archie Cameron, describing his boyhood on Rum before the Great War, remembered when silk shirts waved across the sea to the inhabitants of Canna. Here was held the staff picnic. The food was conveyed from the castle kitchens on horse-drawn carts. Those attending the picnic travelled in "the shining Albions".

What I found was a ruined laundry, a bothy being used by Fiona Guinness who, over many years of research into red deer, beginning in the late 1960s, was able to recognise each deer on sight. When she began her researches, she bestrode the peaty moorland in bare feet. To my surprise, when I was teamed with her in a folk dance during a ceiladh at Kinloch she kicked off her shoes. When she received a much-deserved honorary degree at Edinburgh University, she wore jeans for the occasion.

Last Rites At Harris

*...a tile vault was built, bits of which still show on the bank
behind the lodge, but later a family mausoleum was
constructed in the style of Greek temple.*
Hamish M Brown (1972)

Torrential rain and mist blurred the landmarks on our journey to
Harris. Fortunately we were passengers of the warden and
travelling in a Land Rover. He was intent on feeding some high-
protein "nuts" to the Highland cattle. Good fortune consisted of
having a roof over our heads and some springs beneath us to offset
the rigours of a road that was every bit as rocky as the proverbial road
to Dublin. In the halcyon days just before the Great War, two men
maintained the road system that Sir George had created. On an
island with a high rainfall, the road was subject to wash-outs and new
material to fill in the gaps had to be knapped.

Sir George was involved in the only known road accident, which
occurred at the junction between the Harris and Kilmory roads. He
was driving his Rolls Royce when, taking a bend too fast, it left the
road and came to a halt in a ditch. He summoned George
MacNaughton's help but the Rolls could not be budged. So the
wheels were taken off and it was sledded back on to the road.
Considerable repairs were carried out at the estate workshop.

The bumpy journey through a landscape reduced to various shades
of grey confirmed my opinion of Rum as being the wettest, most
barren in the Small Islands group. As we creaked and rattled along
the eight miles from Kinloch to Harris, I saw deer bounding away.
Two beasts that were tugging coarse grass at a burnside held their
ground. One or two deer wore green collars. When it was reported to
George MacNaughton that a stag was entangled in a net discarded by

fishermen, he would stalk and tranquillise the beast so he could cut away the net. As he left the area, he would look back to check that the stag was back on its feet and grazing.

A red-throated diver occupied a lochan. I retained a special memory of mist, rain, water a shade greyer than the sky and the diver, long and low, like a submarine about to dive. A young conifer plantation had been bleached by salt water during fierce storms. On this day, the Atlantic was grey, choppy, chilling, smothering a weed-strewn beach with milk-white waves. There was a time when the tide brought in a vast number of telegraph poles that had been deck cargo on a freighter, being jettisoned during a severe storm in the Minch.

This south-western corner of Rum was now given over to beasts – to Highland cattle, females with flowing chestnut-red hair and outsweeping horns, and blunt-faced calves at foot. Here, too, were over a score of footloose red deer. As the warden called, the cattle lumbered towards the Land Rover. One was missing. He spotted it in the distance. It was a light-coloured animal with a wee calf. The warden walked through driving rain to feed her – or at least to drop some food nearby. Highland cattle are independent and do not readily accept food from the hand. The red deer were flighty.

The warden told us that red deer and to some extent the cattle dine on seaweed. He had seen goats dining on weed and had found shell-grit in the droppings made by Highland cows. The goats spent most of their time on the cliffs. A kid stranded on a narrow ledge with a sheer drop into the sea could not possibly be rescued. It was shot and fed to the sea eagles. The aforementioned storm, during which the deck-cargo of a freighter in the Minch had to be jettisoned, left the broad sweep of the bay littered with telegraph poles. Most of them lay until they rotted, it being illegal to use them until they had been valued by an inspector appointed by the ship's insurers. No inspector visited the island of Rum.

We turned our attention to the mausoleum erected for three members of the Bullough family – father John, son George and his wife. It was not included in the sale of Rum to the Nature Conservancy, for which they were no doubt thankful. The masonry is exposed to the worst weather the Atlantic can produce. Sir George, who died in 1939, had originally intended that interments would take place in a chamber excavated in a hillside, with ornamental tiles at the entrance. His father was laid to rest here. Then a friend who was shown the place thought the tile-work was in poor taste, reminding him of an urban toilet. George had his father's coffin removed, obliterated the chamber and Daddy was buried at the centre of a field near a shepherd's house. On this spot, in due course, was built a mausoleum in the form of a Doric temple, its roof supported by eighteen columns.

When Lady Bullough died in the South, at a great age, the body was taken to Kinloch Castle. On June 6, 1967, her body was committed to the mausoleum at Harris after an Anglican service there. An unlikely story has persisted that the corpulent body of one who in her young days had been a great beauty was transported to Kinloch Castle. It had been her wish for the coffin to be carried across the island for interment at Harris. The men contrived to move the body by night. It was taken round to Harris surreptitiously by boat, sparing them a gruelling overland journey of eight miles. In truth, Lady Monica appears to have kept a trim figure into her late nineties and – the last link with Rum's most glamorous days – she was borne to her final resting place on the back of a Conservancy Land Rover.

We had a snack meal overlooking Papidil (named after Celtic priests). Sir George had a lodge made here, on the south coast. The building was situated among trees by a freshwater loch. In view, in clear weather, was the island of Muck, Ardnamurchan Point, the most westerly point on the west coast and that curious island known as Dutchman's Cap. (Dutch fishermen were the first to commercially exploit the rich fishery).

A Yorkshire friend who visited Rum when unannounced visits were discouraged, called at the lodge and found the original furnishings, made of white cane, were still *in situ*. The heating system worked so he collected driftwood, stoked up the boiler and had the luxury of a bath within hearing of the sea's roar and under the bemused gaze of wild goats and their kids. They had not previously seen smoke pouring from the building. Another time, a group of Scots was camping nearby. As the sun set, one of them picked up the bagpipes and, marching backwards and forwards, brought tears to everyone's eyes with *Over the Sea to Skye*.

Sea Eagles

Such magnificent creatures were not brought into this world to be held captive; it is especially rewarding to accord them their freedom, knowing that one day some may choose to breed on our long forsaken shores.
John A Love (1983)

On the flats of Harris, Highland cattle were cropping grass and liberally manuring it. The short vegetation was strewn with cast antlers that would be chewed so that the deer might regain some of the lost calcium. A stag that was growing new antlers, protected by the tough hairy skin we call "velvet", was still wearing a tatty winter coat. It would, in due course, be cast as the reddish summer coat grew. Fred said he thought the red deer had been so named because of the blood drawn by stinging insects. From Harris we plodded up a rocky slope, then over mossy ground, displacing a red hind and last year's calf. Swallows were hawking insects at around 2,000 ft.

We were seeking the summit of Ainshval, from which we would descend into Glen Dibidil, returning to Kinloch by the high cliffside path. On Ainshval, the Cuillins of Rum and those of Skye were arrayed before us. Also in view were the smooth grey-blue forms of the Outer Hebrides, like a school of whales, in line ahead. A good sixty miles to the east, Ben Nevis – from this distance a blue smudge – presided over a retinue of lesser hills.

Into view, high above us, riding a thermal in a broad spiral, against an azure sky, was one of the newly-released sea eagles – a youngster, lacking the white tail of the mature bird. This bird was enormous. The wings were straight-edged and the wedge-shaped tail seemed to be attached directly to the trailing edges, as though it was an after-thought.

The Gaelic name for what used to be called the white-tailed sea eagle was *iolair shuil na-greine* – the eagle with the sunlit eye. With its immense wing-span of eight feet, this species has been likened to a flying barn-door. Long years ago, a Northumbrian poet had written "full oft the erne wailed round, spray feathered." *Erne*, a favourite with crossword compilers, is the Anglo Saxon term for this massive bird, meaning "the soarer".

The last pair of sea eagles had nested on Skye in 1916. Nine years before, the last of the breed on Rum had been slain by a gamekeeper. The sea eagle was re-introduced into Britain on Rum, the centre of its former natural range. Hopefully, it would reoccupy some of its old nesting sites which, on the island of Rum, had been adopted by the smaller golden eagle. John Love was caring for fledglings flown from Norway to Kinloss by the RAF under an imaginative scheme of the Nature Conservancy Council.

He had chosen a remote spot and, with minimum disturbance. I felt privileged to accompany him and, from a distance, watch the huge birds tethered on their perches. John was feeding them with whatever came to hand – dead gulls and crows, also mackerel he caught from his small boat. Deer and goat carrion were occasionally on the menu. In due course, the birds would be released into the wild.

John was to chronicle the reintroduction of the species to Rum in his book *The Return of the Sea Eagle*, published in 1983. He took up residence on the island in 1975 and managed the project for the Nature Conservancy Council. The Norwegian authorities gave permission for the export of the first eaglets. It transpired that the RAF made several operational sorties from Kinloss on the Moray Firth to northern Norway. A Nimrod of 120 squadron was enlisted to transport the birds.

The cages were erected on a site overlooking the sea, which would offer ample opportunity for the eagles, on release, to scavenge or hunt along the shore. Over eight seasons, Rum received a total of fifty-five eaglets – thirty females and twenty-five males. On release, an eagle would beat its ponderous wings to gain height and spontaneously discover the basic principles of flight, though one eagle chose to walk out through the open door of its cage and "set off, with a hunched but determined shuffle, to scale a prominent knoll nearby."

(The young of sea eagles nesting on Mull hatch about the tenth of May – alas, a perfect timing for lambing. Fish stocks have declined and there are few rabbits or hares on the ground. Lambs are an easy prey. Yet the islanders have co-operated in schemes to protect the sea eagles. Those who suffer losses have reasonable compensation).

Ashore On Eigg

If I had to choose among the Hebrides... I'd choose Eigg.
Hugh MacDiarmid

My first close encounter with Eigg was en route to Rum. Fifteen miles out of Mallaig, the *Arkaig* hove to near Castle Island and, in the absence of an acceptable jetty or harbour, was attended by the island's *flit boat*, a diesel-powered ferry. I watched with drooping lower jaw as two tons of produce, including cigarettes, cans of beer and bread, were handed over – literally. Three of us joined the chain of workers. Our reward consisted of expressions of thanks and the unanimous vote of the crew that we should have a hundred per cent discount on the fare from Mallaig to Rum.

The attitude of the conventional tourists taking the regulation trip between Mallaig and Oban was amusing to watch, especially – as one old-time visitor noted – "the steamer slows down at Eigg and prepares to receive the ferry boat. Women, fashionably clad in garments quite unsuited to the Highlands, and some of the men little less absurdly dressed, cluster round the rails and wonder who can possibly be going to land in such rough fashion at such an unheard-of place.

"The sailors throw our luggage into the boat as though it were rubbish of which the steamer was well rid and, truth to tell, our traps – from long experience of similar treatment – do look as if they had seen better days. We tumble down on the top of our belongings and push off from the steamer under the pitying glance of the passengers, who are obviously thanking their stars that they are at least bound for a place mentioned in every guide book."

Robert Atkinson, who explored the north-western isles of Scotland, searching for shearwaters and petrels, landed on Eigg in the

1930s and wrote: "The day before yesterday I had been a hundred and fifty miles northward, in the far harsh desolation of Rona, milling with sea-fowl under a dirty white sky. Today Eigg lay in southern summer hat and the white road was dusty." I read elsewhere that the folk on Eigg called the shearwater a puffin.

The gamekeeper once dug from a burrow "the great fat baby bird" so that a visiting lady might see it properly. The chick, of placid temperament, did not stir at the treatment. Some quaint ideas circulated, such as the shearwater's inclination latterly to feed sorrel leaves, not fish, to its fledgling. "So, in order that it may be able, first to get out of its hole, which it fills completely, then to fly, the baby bird has to submit to a course of reducing diet."

Eigg, a fair and lovely island, got its second "g" as recently as the nineteenth century. The name does not relate to eggs. It is derived from a Gaelic word for The Notch, a central V-shaped glen, marking the division between a gee-whiz feature variously known as Sgurr or Scurr and moorland to the north. Striated vertically, this immense lump of rock, capped by a block of pitchstone porphyry, tickles passing clouds at 1,289 ft. It has been described as standing haughtily aloof with a suggestion of superiority over the moorland.

The black mass of the Sgurr creates a micro-climate in its lee and, with a virtual absence of frosts, leads to a rich and varied vegetation – including palm trees and eucalyptus. One day, when cuckoos were lively, I heard a succession of double *cuck-oos* as a bird's calling had a responsive echo from the cliffs.

I landed on Eigg with friends. We carried our heavy packs through daisy-covered fields to the Manse, where the Missionary's wife provided us with coffee. The evening meal consisted of celery and rice soup, stew and mashed potatoes, followed by rhubarb with cream and cups of strong tea. The Missionary had been born on the Long Island, as the outer group was known. He told us that his aged mother wrote regularly to him. "She thinks in Gaelic but writes letters in English."

Then we went on a journey of exploration, beginning with a ruined kirk and a Celtic cross with a top propped against the base. "Och," said an islander, "it was in the way of a flash of lightning." We came across a plastic sack and thought to do the (only) local shopkeeper a favour by collecting some of the hundreds of beer cans that lay within throwing distance of traffic on the (only) road. When we handed the sack to her, she came close to tears. Taking us to the back of the shop she pointed out a mini-mountain of rusty cans.

It was, as usual, a fine Easter – but cold, painting frost-pictures on the window of the attic room in which George and I were quartered. We decided not to undress but to clamber as we were into bed. In the morning, George looked out of the window, expecting to see ice floes in the sound.

So much for the sunny side of Eigg; in the west, mist boiled over the Cleadale cliffs like steam rising from a cauldron, obscuring the island of Rum and giving the voices of ravens a sinister sound. Eigg was a floral island, not yet stung by agricultural sprays. It held a profusion of primroses, orchids and, at high levels, patches of moss campion.

George proposed we climb the Sgurr, though viewed from the Manse it presented a range of unscalable cliffs. "Och, nae problem," said George and promptly led us round the back, where a track led us to a gully (or could it have been the celebrated notch?) by which we gained the summit ridge. A rusting metal bar was an eyesore but consoled a villager who used it as a reflector for a television set for one of the villagers. When we passed a house, the familiar H aerial was being overhauled; taken down, it was being attended to using strips of adhesive tape.

John, who had been unusually quiet, decided to seek medical help from Hector MacLean, who had been doctoring the Small Islands, with a base on Eigg, since 1951. Edwin Waugh, visiting the Small Isles in Victorian days, wrote that there was a doctor on Eigg but none on Rum. The exception was "one or two wild-eyed herdsmen who know how to tinker up the sheep and kine when they are ailing; and the old women… who are, amongst themselves, what the lowland Scotch call 'doctors by guess'."

The doctor's home-cum-surgery sought by John was a modern bungalow. John rapped on the door and was confronted by Hector, a stocky man wearing the kilt. He fixed John with a lingering stare, then declared: "What you need is – *fresh air!*" And that was that. The most common ailment he dealt with occurred in springtime and was known as the Eigg bug. The sufferer lost condition rapidly through diarrhoea and sickness. Then, suddenly, normality was regained.

Alcoholism was common before the days of television, which provided a "window on the world". We associated it with what we called "winter sickness", our name for attacks of morbidity and depression experienced by people living on remote northern islands when the old culture had broken down and the population declined. They became broody through the short days and long dark nights, when there was just the crackling radio and the whine of the wind for company. Some found release through wee drams.

It was on Eigg that George demonstrated his ability to light a fire with a single match and sandwich paper, using fish boxes and debris picked up from a beach being swept by heavy rain. We were near the Singing Sands having walked up through Cleadale, where an old man told us how his family cooked shearwaters. Sheltering from the rain under an overhang on the main cliff, we consumed our food. "Och, but let's have a fire," said George. We watched enthralled as he crumpled the sandwich paper. Then, picking up part of a fish box, he used his knife to produced fine shavings of wood, which he carefully spread over the paper. So fine were the shavings, they soon caught fire. The size and bulk of material was increased as the fire took hold. In a frenzy of tidiness we picked up plastic objects and incinerated them.

The Singing Sands, which we now explored, utter their shrill squeaking when the grains, which are uniform in size, have been dampened. They were not in a vocal mood that day. Hugh Miller, in *The Cruise of the Betsy*, published in 1858, was the first person to make the sands sing in prose. He recalled striking the sand obliquely with a foot, where the surface lay dry, "and elicited a shrill sonorous note." He repeated the action. With every blow the shrill note was repeated. My companion joined me: and we performed a concert which, if we could boast of but little variety in the tones produced, might at least challenge all Europe for an instrument of the kind which produced them."

Robert Atkinson, of pleasant memory, was shearwatering on Eigg in 1937 when, for four days, "the remarkable thing that happened was a heat wave." He and his friends "splashed in and out of the not unwarm sea…slept in the sun or shuffled bare feet into the hot sand, the Singing Sand, and made it produce its unnatural squeaks and grunts. Blue sky, hazy sky pale and hot, not a soul about."

The Missionary was a sociable man who joined us in the evening and contrived to smoke cigarettes and imbibe whisky from the day's bottle opened by "the lads". He happily combined his religious duties with something akin to crofting, using the church's few acres.

We arrived on Eigg a day after a new owner, Keith Shellenberg, had taken over, spectacularly, landing his private aircraft on a cliff-top grassy strip. We met him as we sauntered through the sheltered grounds of The Lodge, a twelve-bedroomed house of Italianate style, commissioned by Lord Walter Runciman, shipping magnate (and cabinet minister), designed by Balfour Paul, an architect with a practice based on Newcastle and completed in 1927.

Runciman was born in 1870, the same year as Sir George Bullough. He could afford to make The Lodge impressive for he had bought Eigg for £15,000. The Lodge, like Kinloch Castle on Rum and the big-hoose on Canna, had a grand piano. A piano-tuner from the mainland attended to each piano in turn. Like Bullough, his lordship wanted a sporting estate. Eigg had a quite large community of crofters so red deer would have been inappropriate. The sport on Eigg was with pheasants, up to four thousand birds being set free annually. How many ended their lives in crofters' cooking pots is not recorded.

At the time we sauntered through the grounds of The Lodge, we were under the impression it was awaiting its new owner. What could have been a nasty case of trespass in wooded grounds that were originally based on those at Inverewe, in north-west Scotland, turned out to be an affable re-union of Yorkshiremen. He had bought Eigg when, while yachting round the islands, he had an impulse to own one of them. He purchased the seven thousand acres of Eigg in December 1974 for £265,000 and took possession on April 1st in the following year. Shellenberg hoped that his romantic enthusiasm and ideas would breathe new life into a community of forty, most of them living on crofts. The landing craft he had built, at a cost of £15,000, was for the use of the islanders with animals they needed to transport to the mainland.

Another time, I was in the company of Fred. It was, as ever, springtime. The island, which can be dour at winter, seemed lovelier than ever in the dry, warm conditions, with the sun burning its way through mist to reveal a turquoise sea lapping against white sands. Bluebells provided the dominant hue along the cliff edges. We spotted our old friend, *Loch Arkaig*, on its second round of the Small Isles that day – a small boat in a big sea.

As we crossed the island, heading for the Cleadale cliffs, we saw saxifrages in a marshy area. Also thousands of orchids. Bluebells were so profuse many of them grew among heather, hinting at the old wooded state of the island. On the high cliffs were two of the gee-whiz plants – mountain avens and moss campion, the former in profusion and in full flower, with the "fried egg" effect on the petals of yellow ringed by white.

In the old days, when the folk of Eigg lived off what they could grow or catch, shearwaters appeared on the menu. So many were eaten the folk were named after the Gaelic word for shearwater, which is falach. Each March, the birds arrived from their wintering grounds and occupied burrows on the cliffs above Cleadale. The crofters – like many island folk – were in part "bird people", gathering up fat young birds, skinning them and boiling them "like haggis". Some birds were eaten immediately. Others, salted down, were stored for winter consumption. Stewed shearwater was a regular winter dish. Few remain. Rats, otters and hungry folk decimated the colony.

Eigg was attractive to cuckoos. That year, the first of the spring arrivals had been heard on May 1, which was later than usual. Three cuckoos were seen in flight. One alighted on a telegraph pole. The evenings were punctuated by cuckooing, with one bird noticeably off-key.

Mission To Muck

...very fertile and fruitful of cornes and grassing for all store
and very good fishing ...a good falcon nest on it.
Sir Donald Munro (1549)

On Sunday morning the Missionary went out to milk his cow, taking his radio with him so as to listen to the weather forecast. That day he planned to take a service on the isle of Muck. He had hired the craft from the doctor's son, who normally used it for fishing. And so it was that the doctor had free passage in order to attend his few patients on Muck, whether or not they needed attention.

The Missionary wore a raven-black suit. His young daughter had donned an outfit of soft russet tints, complete with bonnet. The doctor, Hector Maclean, wore his kilt with the obligatory dirk tucked into one of his stockings. I was told that his Scottishness extended to a fondness for playing the pipes. Hector had the normal problems of an island doctor and responsibilities for the three other islands in the group. In emergency, he might summon the lifeboat or a helicopter. This occurred on Eigg when two of the island cars collided on the island's only road.

We left Eigg in a flurry of sea-foam and with a dinghy bobbing in our wake. After a brief dallance with the open sea, we approached Port Mor, on Muck. The name was said to be an anglicised version of the Gaelic for "sea pig", possibly an allusion to migrant dolphin or to the grey seals that haul themselves up in quite places for pupping.

I hoped the rope connecting us to the dinghy was securely tied for ahead was white water. The horizontal terracing of the basalt extended offshore as two reefs, Bogha Ruadh and Dubh Sheir, and our way lay between them. The boatman, staying well out, followed the line of the shore until the gable end of a particular cottage appeared to view from behind a low cliff. This was our marker. We headed directly towards it with the sea boiling and bubbling around us. The final approach, on calmer water, was under the gaze of cormorant, shag, eider and black guillemot.

Muck, the smallest of the island group, a mere three miles of basaltic rock, seemed to be having a struggle to keep above water level. Volcanic laval had broken down into good soil. With a mild climate, Muck had an enviable reputation for early potatoes. Between the wars, the MacEwen family, who had owned the island since 1879, gave it a pastoral character, introducing cattle and exporting cheese. They also planted trees.

While the Missionary gathered his "flock" we walked through the Deserted Village, a roofless complex because, having been created by displaced crofters early in the nineteenth century, it had been inexplicably vacated. Cheviot sheep with lambs at foot grazed the spring flush of grass. As we ate our snack meal on a knoll above the white-sand beach near Horse Island, we espied the Eigg doctor, a solitary figure taking a short cut across the low-tide sands.

Fred, spying a telephone kiosk, put in a transfer call to his wife in Ben Rhydding, Yorkshire. He heard her voice, followed by that of the operator inquiring if she was prepared to pay for a call from Muck. Said Fred's wife, Vera, who had never heard of Muck, "I beg your pardon..."

On the return to Eigg, we carried two boxes of chickens, one box for the Missionary and the other for the doctor. As Fred observed: "It's a real chicken and Eigg situation." The boxes were crisp and firm as the voyage began but a frisky breeze blew exhaust vapour across the boat, some of it settling as moisture on the boxes. As they were lifted from the boat at Eigg, a slow collapse began. Next morning, at 6.15, I awoke at the Manse to crowing and a fluttering sound from the hen run. Fresh chickens were introducing themselves to the Manse flock with prolonged and noisy rites.

Craking On Canna

We left Canna in a flood of yellow evening sunshine; it had been a fine day!
Robert Atkinson (1936)

As the ferry approached Canna, a girl wearing fashionable clothes and with a modern hair style mentioned that she was visiting her father, who had a job on the island. I asked her what he did. The girl looked to where waves broke their backs on naked rock, beyond which were basalt plateaux, thatched with coarse grass. She replied: "God knows." To be fair to Canna, it does have imposing sea cliffs, including the 690 ft. drop at Carn a Gahaill, also Compass Hill, where iron in the rock was said to play games with the compass of a passing ship. There is also a tract of woodland.

On one of my Small Isles voyages, George pointed out the lone figure of John Lorne Campbell. A much-respected student of Gaelic culture, Campbell had bought Canna in 1938. He had his head in a book and I could not pluck up courage to disturb him with what was bound to be a triviality. Campbell was a great friend of the novelist Compton Mackenzie, who lived on The Long Island. In 1933, they founded the Sea League to preserve the Minch for native fishermen. Campbell and his wife, Margaret Fay Shaw, a scholar of Gaelic literature and culture, had no heirs. The island was given to the National Trust for Scotland.

Despite its small size and bleak appearance, Canna had the only jetty on the Small Isles. The name *Cana* means porpoise. We had glimpsed some of these sleek creatures on the voyage from Rum. Now the ferry's propeller stirred the sea into milky-white. A black guillemot that had been floating like a buoy dived in a stretch of clear water, showing off its red legs, and adding yet more bubbles to what was otherwise a gin-clear sea.

Robert Atkinson, in *Island Going*, described his visits "to the remoter isles, chiefly uninhabited, off the North-West corner of Scotland" in the 1930s. He was recommended to visit Canna for its shearwaters and after crossing the Sea of the Hebrides "in darkness and rain the steamer approached a small wooden pier lit by two or three storm lanterns. We got off – no one else – and a flock of sheep was urged to get in. The mailboat slid away; various men went off swinging their lanterns. We remained with our heap of luggage in the wet darkness. The road or track from the pier was a pale strip of rutted mud leading faintly into the unknown. We pitched the tent on a sodden patch of long grass."

Now, forty years later, Fred and I disembarked to be spattered by the first large drops of rain heralding a storm. They sent us scuttering into a Presbyterian Church that was visited by the Missionary from Eigg one, sometimes twice, a year. This unusual building, fashioned of grey stones, with its conspicuous round tower, Irish style, looked half as old as time but was opened for worship in 1914. In marked contrast, a huge Catholic Church dominated the Sanday shore. This church, built in the 1890s by the 3rd Marquess of Bute, was somewhat inconvenient. Services were resumed in St Columba's chapel on Canna. At the time of my visit, the two faiths collaborated in an unusual respect. Each week, one of the Catholic community, just before catching the ferry, called at the Presbyterian church, took the money from the collection plate and deposited it in its special account at a bank in Mallaig.

We had hired a quite large house, standing in capacious grounds near the bridge linking Canna with Sanday. Reaching our quarters involved walking and wading, a section of the track having been overswept by the tide. The diversion was across the edge of a marshy field. The bedrooms we occupied were far enough apart for us to be out of snoring range. The peat-tinted water that gushed from the taps looked like pale ale. We had the use of a Rayburn stove, fed with driftwood from the beach and coal brought in by "puffer" from the Clyde.

Our first meal was afternoon tea, at the invitation of Mary Anne, alias Herself, from whom we rented the house. Aged 77, and with a regal appearance, Mary Anne was a Gaelic speaker who, when she used English, did so with a fine regard for diction. She had style. We found her wearing Sunday best and using her finest china cups. Each plate in the matching set held a piece of Lyon's Swiss-roll. Mary Anne had decided views about current affairs. She spoke nostalgically about the old days and asserted "there are no Highland gentlemen left."

Back at the bothy, Fred put together a meal consisting of steak and kidney pies, somewhat squashed after the sea journey, powdered potato, tinned beans, sliced bread and soft margarine. I sauntered back to the village, looking for a telephone kiosk, which turned out to be painted blue, not red, with a door hanging off, having been vandalised by the weather. I met a party of Scottish schoolboys who, with several teachers, were on a bird-watching holiday.

My bird-watching had begun with long vigils near a bird haunt or nest. I would peer at the birds through binoculars, then record what I had seen in a diary. The lads had been infused with modern ideas, being provided with torches for dazzling shearwaters, hooks for grabbing nesting shags for "ringing" and a tape-recording of a male corncrake to entice a local bird. In between the bird and the tape-recorder was set a mist net. When we told the boys we had found a beached shark, their first impulse was to grab a hammer to knock out some teeth as souvenirs.

We watched birds in the old-fashioned way, through binoculars, from a distance. Eight raven gavorted in the sky. One flipped over on its back, then righted itself, as though for the sheer joy of living. Fred almost stepped on the nest of a pair of snipe; it held four eggs. A fulmar petrel cruised by on wings held out so stiff that they might have been made of balsa wood. A ringed plover scurried on the beach. When it suddenly stopped, it was difficult to pick it out against a beach of assorted patterns and tones. We saw a dunlin in full breeding attire.

At 9.40, the "edge o' dark", a cuckoo uttered a lullaby. At 10.00, a freckle-faced schoolboy rapped on the door and invited us to join a "craking" party. We repaired with them to a meadow where the tape-recorder and mist net had already been set up. By now it was dark. The recorded voice of a corncrake sounded tinny. Years ago, I had simulated the bird's call by grating a comb on a matchbox. On Canna, the local male came to investigate. When it was just short of the mist net, it turned and walked away. And that was that. Back at the house, I awoke from sleep to hear the *crex, crex* of a corncrake. From the window, I saw the island had been plated with silver by a new moon. Moonlight and the sound of a lazy tide smacking its lips on the nearby beach gave the corncrake's presence a special quality.

Next day, on the eastern heights of Canna, almost seven hundred feet above the restless sea, the air was so clear, having been storm-washed, that we saw the Outer Hebrides as a line of blue hummocks. At their nearest point they were over thirty miles away. South Uist lies twenty-four miles from Canna. Fred was sure we could identify Harris – which, at a rough calculation on the map, lies at a range of sixty miles.

At night, in the company of our young friends, we went "shear-watering", with moderate success. Robert Atkinson had been advised to seek out Mr MacIsaac, who knew all about these birds. He was a cheerful, rubicund man, full of good tales. Once, when he had been ferreting and listening at a rabbit hole, a shearwater appeared and nipped his ear. He took them to the very bank, riddled with holes, where he had his ear tweaked years before. The visit was in wild weather. Next day they returned to the sodden ground with a spade and dug into the burrows, finding they "branched deeper and deeper into labyrinths". Yet the inside of the bank was dry. "The tail end of the gale blew earth into our eyes and ears and mouths." The nearest Robert Atkinson and his friends got to the shearwaters were some dead remains and a dirty old egg.

We crossed a footbridge to what used to be the tidal island of Sanday – the old Sand Island – where the few crofters used to spend more time fishing for cod and lobster rather than tilling the ground. We found ourselves under the unblinking gaze of several grey seals, close to the shore. An eighty-year-old crofter had been so long in the outdoors his face looked as though it had been carved from mahogany. He wore almost as much wool as a sheep. The hat, pullover and long stockings looked home-knitted and his mackintosh had a length of twine as a belt. His footwear consisted of wellingtons, only one of which was fully visible. One of the trouser legs obscured the other.

A woman visitor had miraculously located rhubarb in the overgrown garden of the last occupied crofting house. Miss Mary Flora Steele, out gathering driftwood, reported seeing a particularly large piece of what she thought was plastic lying on dark rocks a few hundred yards away. Fred scanned it through his binoculars and said: "It's a bloody whale!" It was indeed a bloody shark, aforementioned. We estimated it was over twenty feet long and weighed perhaps three tons.

As we reached the cliffs, we espied tysties. Five birds were in one group, well away from the shore. We stalked a cuckoo and walked through a small gullery. Tons of driftwood, including telegraph poles (from the jettisoned deck-cargo of the storm-wracked ship) occupied a deep gully. An oystercatcher, while harrying a hooded crow, collided with it. Fred, who was virtually underneath at the time, reported hearing the thump.

Homeward Bound

We returned to Mallaig on a sun-dappled sea, as if nature had stopped trying to impress us with its more violent aspects. The voyage was on the *Arkaig*, though she would not remain on the Small Isles run for much longer and would be replaced by a modern vessel. Ian, the ferryman, his open boat laden with our party and our possessions, awaited *Arkaig* as she sailed into Loch Scresort.

Earlier that day, I ventured to the castle and pondered on its decline. The Great War brought its glory days to an end. The fabulous Edwardian period, and the great days of Rum as a sporting estate, ended with the clash of arms. The Bulloughs remained solvent, belying an old Lancashire saying of third generation profligacy – "clogs to clogs in three generations." The outbreak of war in 1914 led to the estate being put on a care and maintenance basis. Men of fighting age were called up for war service. Most of them did not return. Sir George was raised to the baronetcy in 1916 for giving the Government an interest-free loan of £50,000.

When peace of a sort was re-established, he and his wife visited Rum for brief periods only. The magic had gone. They tried to recover the spirit of Edwardian times but the grounds had declined and labour was scarce. One of the casualties of war had been the old social system. Afterwards, when Sir George and his wife, with a smaller staff, visited Rum, they used the mailboat. As the years passed, glasshouses decayed and weeds had the upper hand in what had been immaculate gardens. The tropical birds were no more. Turtles, released into the sea, soon perished in an unfamiliar environment.

Hermione, the only child of Sir George and Lady Bullough, married the Earl of Durham in 1932. Sir George had a fatal heart attack while playing golf near Boulogne in the summer of 1939. His bride of long years joined shooting parties on Rum after the Second World War. In 1954, aged eighty-five, she paid her last visit to Rum. She died in 1967, aged ninety-eight, and her mortal remains were taken to join those of her husband and father-in-law in the mausoleum at Harris, by the lonely Atlantic shore.

The Globe Works at Accrington, once the workplace of 5,000 people, have ceased to exist, though the office block is now the Globe Centre. The enterprise that evolved from a partnership between James Bullough and John Howard in 1856 throve through its drive and inventiveness. They revolutionised the textile industry. Howard and Bullough exported a range of modern machinery to lands overseas. The recipients put their machines to such good use they provided stiff opposition to a Lancashire cotton industry that was still using unimproved models. In due course, the firm suffered the historic fate of mergers and reorganisations which, at the time of my visit in 1993, led to the premises looking dowdy.

Rum, so remote in spirit from the mills, back-to-back houses and stone setts of industrialised Lancashire, provided the Bulloughs with social standing and sporting opportunities. Rum was to pass into the ownership of the Nature Conservancy Council and is now administered under the Scottish Parliament.

Memories of Rum endure. In my mind's eye I can still see the Sound of Sleet, silvered by summer sunshine, and I am briefly entertained by thoughts of characterful men like Brucie Watts and the shearwaters. A bird rises, turns on its side, shows its white underparts, then follows a deep trough between waves, rising again, wings stiffly outstretched, taking the uplift of wind from the waves. I recall seeing two rafts of shearwaters totalling several hundred birds. When it was dark, they would fly to burrows on the mountain tops and rend the chilly Hebridean air with their yodelling calls…

Also from Castleberg –

REGINALD FARRER

The "father" of rock gardening was born in London, was reared at a mansion in the limestone country of north-west Yorkshire and died in the wilds of Burma. He is remembered not so much for his odd appearance and eccentricities but as a plant-collector who ranged over Europe and Asia, introducing over a hundred species that were new to British gardens.

ISBN : 1 871064 43 0   £5.99

KIT CALVERT

With his floppy trilby, his grizzle-grey hair and clay pipe, Kit stood out in a crowd. He was the sage of Hawes, the saviour of the Wensleydale cheese industry, a translator of passages from the Bible into local dialect and the owner of a most unusual bookshop.

ISBN : 1 871064 38 4   £5.99

CASTLEBERG BOOKS
18 Yealand Avenue, Giggleswick, Settle, North Yorkshire, BD24 0AY